THE STERLING YEARS

THE
STERLING YEARS

Small-arms and the men

by
James Edmiston

Pen & Sword
MILITARY

First published in Great Britain in 1992 by
LEO COOPER

Reprinted in this format in 2011 by
Pen & Sword Military
an imprint of
Pen & Sword Books Ltd
47 Church Street
Barnsley
South Yorkshire   S70 2AS

ISBN 978 1 84884 437 7

Printed and bound in England
by CPI Antony Rowe, Chippenham, Wiltshire

Pen & Sword Books Ltd incorporates the imprints of
Pen & Sword Aviation, Pen & Sword Maritime, Pen & Sword Military,
Wharncliffe Local History, Pen & Sword Select,
Pen & Sword Military Classics and Leo Cooper,
Remember When, Seaforth Publishing and Frontline Publishing

For a complete list of Pen & Sword titles please contact
PEN & SWORD BOOKS LIMITED
47 Church Street, Barnsley, South Yorkshire, S70 2AS, England
E-mail: enquiries@pen-and-sword.co.uk
Website: www.pen-and-sword.co.uk

This book is dedicated to the staff and workforce of the Sterling Armament Company Ltd, of whose loyalty I have yet to find the equal, and also to those countries who had the good sense to adopt the Sterling sub-machine gun.

CONTENTS

FOREWORD

This is a cautionary tale of one man's experiences in the small-arms industry – mine. It is the story of how I acquired and subsequently lost the Sterling Armament Company, at considerable personal and financial cost, thanks to the dishonesty, jealousy and hypocrisy of others. It is an explanation of how I came to believe, as I now do, that the day of the truly private military arms manufacturer is over, even in America.

The arms trade is an emotive subject, and small-arms especially so. The gun-worshipper who opens this book with eager hands will find no songs of praise from me. I am proud to have been associated with the manufacture of probably the most reliable automatic firearm ever made, the Sterling sub-machine gun, but this does not mean that I find anything intrinsically glamorous about guns. As pieces of fine engineering they do possess an aesthetic appeal, at least to those who can appreciate such skills, yet the essential fascination derives from their potency as weapons. Whether or not it is true that the assassin's bullet has ever altered the course of history, there remains the possibility that it might.

Still less glamorous is the actual trading aspect. The scenery might be exotic and beautiful, the sums of money involved might be huge, but the traders or 'fixers' have to keep a very clear head when dealing with buyers. The risks are high. Double-dealing and corruption may lurk in wait, even behind the most charming and dependable façade – even, alas, within the British Government.

It is not my intention however, to point out governmental incompetence, or to underline the waste of money and effort involved on a national level, or to suggest that British hypocrisy over procurement practices is any worse than in other countries. It is merely my wish, in writing this book, to set the record straight for The Sterling Years.

CHAPTER ONE

Quite a Good Shot

My first experience of shooting was with a .22″ Martini rifle in the air-raid shelter that housed a rifle range, down by the River Cherwell. I was 11 years old and at the Dragon School, Oxford. There was a real attraction to me, then, of carrying a firearm and having the trappings of a soldier. Sadly, the practice was stopped − not out of any fear for security, but rather because one of the young lads managed to sneak out a live round and then despatched an unfortunate mallard.

After the Dragon School I went to Rugby School in Warwickshire. My father had been a rugby player of some renown, and it was because the game had originated at the school that he chose to send me there. Though I never matched my father's standard, I enjoyed rugby. I did not like cricket, though, and so during the summers, in order to avoid it, I followed my father's advice and took up shooting. Now it was a Lee Enfield .303″ that I strapped to my back for the cycle ride through town to the Brownsover ranges, today part of a housing estate.

I considered myself quite a good shot, but somehow lacked the right temperament. Sheer excitement sometimes made me ruin my own chances. In a match, when everything hung on the last shot, my unsteady breathing or simple lack of concentration would make me spoil things with a 'magpie', a wild shot. Still, I did join the clutch of likely candidates for the shooting VIII one summer for the warm-up week at Bisley, and so experienced the delights of the Mecca of the shooting world. The heady moment soon passed. Perhaps it was the sun that sapped my concentration, but Regimental Sergeant-Major Bates despaired of my shooting and I was out of the team.

Meanwhile, however, I had discovered a new dodge. In the swimming matches against other schools there was always a diving event that carried an inordinate number of points towards the match. It had occurred to me that jumping around on a trampolene or a spring-board was a hell of a sight easier than flogging down to Brownsover with a heavy rifle on my back. Therefore I now changed over to swimming – or, more correctly, diving. I'm almost ashamed to admit it, but I was in the school swimming VIII for two years without swimming a stroke.

Whilst at school we all had to join a 'voluntary' combined cadet force, affiliated to the Royal Warwickshire Regiment. On occasions we were sent on exercise and issued with rifles and a few blank rounds of ammunition. The local stationers must have made a fortune, since half the school was firing pencils around the Warwickshire countryside. But there was a considerable gap before I touched a gun again. I now spent an idyllic (and idle) three years at Oxford reading law – at Brasenose College, as it happens, where William Webb Ellis had gone before. It was Ellis who, with a fine disregard for the rules of football as played in his time, picked up and ran with the ball during a schoolboy match at Rugby and so invented the game. There are no records as to his further participation in either rugby or association football, but when he went on to Oxford he won a blue for playing cricket for the University against Cambridge.

During my time at Brasenose I played rugby on three occasions against a team from the Honourable Artillery Company. This most individualistic organization was (and still is) a territorial army unit situated on the northern borders of the City of London. Founded in 1537, it is technically the oldest regiment in the British Army. It had fought as a unit in the South African and First World Wars, as an old friend of my father's recalled while lunching with me at Armoury House, the Regimental Headquarters. During the Great War he had seen HAC batteries bringing their horse-drawn artillery into position and then saw them being picked off, one by one, by the German artillery. The losses were appalling. In the Second World War the regiment became officer-producing. In fact, some would have me believe that it still is.

Having gone down from Oxford I went one day to watch Brasenose play the HAC on their most valuable ground in the City.

Apparently it had been a burial ground for victims of the Great Plague in 1665, and the rugby team spread the rumour that anyone who suffered so much as a graze would require an immediate tetanus jab. Some of the HAC players recognized me from past games and were most welcoming. Thereafter I received frequent invitations to dine at Armoury House until eventually, feeling myself under something of an obligation, I picked up my boots again to play rugby for the HAC team.

In fact I ended up joining the Territorial Army. My decision to do so was only partly influenced by the fact that, if I was playing rugby for the regiment whilst technically attending a military week-end, I was paid full army pay as a private – or, in my case, a gunner. That was the nearest I came to playing professional sport.

In the summer of 1970, our rugby-playing adjutant, Captain J. H. (Jimmy) James, late of the Coldstream Guards, pulled off an amazing coup: he was instrumental in organizing the regiment's two-week summer camp in Cyprus. The stories surrounding those 14 days are legion, but for me there were three high spots. They included the skydiving, even though it resulted for me in a badly broken leg. Before that I'd also enjoyed the pleasures of a weekend in the then luxury and splendour of Beirut in the Lebanon. But perhaps the most significant experience of the fortnight was the morning spent on the range firing the L2A3, more commonly known as the Sterling sub-machine gun. That little lightweight gun of outstanding mechanical beauty gave me an enormous sense of power, especially when shooting from the hip in the full automatic mode, throwing up clouds of dust on the range. It was only a brief encounter, but the memory will remain with me until my dying day.

A year later I bought the company.

CHAPTER TWO

A Star is Born

During my last term at Oxford I had been told that I would make a good country solicitor. It was wise advice, but I took it completely the wrong way. To me it meant that I would never make a decent barrister. At the time I'd been eating dinners at the Middle Temple, along with assorted citizens of the Commonwealth, and I had always assumed that one day I would be there not as a candidate but as a member in my own right. The man who thus dashed my hopes of a career at the Bar was my tutor, R. H. (Ron) Maudsley who, as I ought to have realized, was genuinely trying to help. A handsome and sociable man but a rather reluctant academic, in the space of four terms after the end of the Second World War he had achieved two firsts (Bachelor of Arts and Bachelor of Civil Law) and three blues (cricket, golf and fives), and was about to take over the running of the Shell operation in Shanghai when Mao Tse-tung and the Communists intervened in 1949. With his ability and outgoing nature he would have made an outstanding success of the operation, and the cloistered life must have seemed somewhat narrow in comparison. So when Ron talked about country solicitors it sounded as though he was recommending a career of mediocre obscurity.

Indignant, I vowed to have nothing further to do with law. I just wish I'd been able to keep to my vow.

The question then arose of what else I could do. My father had been a member of the Worshipful Company of Horners – the name derives from the fact that they once made combs, beakers, spoons etc. from horn; now the material is plastic – and I had developed an interest in plastics too. A regular reader of *Plastics and Rubber Weekly* (not a porno but a trade magazine), I began to sense a gap in the market. What the industry needed was a mould-making facility. The idea took shape, and soon my next step was clear. I had to start up or otherwise acquire an engineering company. After months of scouring the pages of the *Financial Times*, I eventually found a sub-contract engineering firm in the hands of a receiver.

It was plain enough to see what had gone wrong. Two partners had been a bit heavy-handed with the remuneration and business lunches and a touch too *laissez-faire* where profitability was concerned. But it was easy for me to criticize; I had no kids to educate and no wife barking about bills to be paid.

In 1968, about the time that I joined the HAC, I bought the engineering firm. I had explained my mould-making idea to the bank and they loaned me the full purchase price, asking only that I provide a bank guarantee. I was still struggling to pay the battels (college bill) at this stage – my last year at Oxford had proven woefully expensive – and was grateful when my mother agreed to help. She willingly offered to provide the bank guarantee on condition that 40% of the equity went to my younger brother, then still at school. None of us could have foreseen what significance this would have later.

I can't claim single-handed responsibility for the first few years' success, though I worked hard enough. Really the man responsible was Gerry Schreiber, the works director. Formerly a regimental sergeant-major in the Royal Engineers, Gerry had enjoyed his war so much – so he once told me – that on VE Day, when hostilities ended, he had even shed a tear or two. Between us, and ably assisted by others, we soon had the facility up and running. The total investment was covered by the net profit made in the first year; and in the second year all the tax losses were used up.

Fired with success, I wooed and married my wife in 1970. The wedding took place in South Africa, at Tzaneen in the northern Transvaal, with me hobbling down the aisle on crutches, my leg pieced together with bolts and screws and encased in plaster up the hip. It was just a couple of months since my skydiving experience in Cyprus. Taking an extended honeymoon, we toured Rhodesia, Mozambique and Swaziland, with me driving a suitably adapted yellow Volkswagen with my left foot.

Back in England in 1971, we bought a house in Chelsea. A new wife, a new home: I soon realized it was time to expand operations at the engineering firm. We needed a new end product or acquisition. I resolved to keep my eyes and ears open – never expecting to find what I wanted so soon or in such odd circumstances.

One of the selling points of the house in Chelsea was the continuity of the cleaning lady's services: Mrs Waller. Her family is well known to Londoners as they are the flower-sellers in Belgrave Square. We shared May Waller's services with another lady and one day, when May arrived for work looking downcast, my wife discovered that the other lady's boy friend had just died in an air crash. The boy friend, it turned out, had been Clive Raphael, a property developer.

Curious, I looked into what he had owned. His main asset had been the control of Land & General Developments Ltd, a property company with two subsidiary holdings, one to do with greetings cards and the other engineering. The engineering subsidiary consisted of three separate companies. One, called Caslake, made centralizers for the oil industry. The second was Russell Newbury, which made large long-stroke, slow-running diesel engines, ideal for generators and pumping engines, and for marine auxiliaries. And the third company was the Sterling Armament Company.

Naturally it was Sterling that interested me, because most of the manufacturing processes were similar to those used in my own engineering firm. But the property market was at a high and I thought I stood a chance of acquiring the whole Land & General operation. Obtaining bank support to put in a bid and thinking myself very clever, I called a board meeting. Every property shark in London was after the company, and the directors looked at me in complete bemusement when I announced my intention.

The central problem was that all the owners of the voting shares had died in the air crash: Clive Raphael himself, his father and another passenger. He had acquired Land & General and shortly thereafter sold a quantity of Sterling sub-machine guns to the Malaysian government and then bought the Beagle aircraft with the proceeds of this sale. He was piloting it himself, on his way to France, when the wings iced up and the Beagle crashed. All on board were killed.

There were other problems too, involving Raphael's will. To his estranged wife, the gorgeous model Penny Brahms, he had left the princely sum of one shilling and four photographs of herself nude. The will was contested and odd lawyers and secretaries disappeared with the police hard on their heels; even Raphael's white Rolls-Royce disappeared.

It was, in short, all rather a mess. But at some stage the voting problems would have to be resolved and I wanted to state my interest in advance. I told the assembled board of directors that I'd be more than happy to settle for just the Sterling Armament Company, and I made my bid. In my innocence I thought it would help if they had a concrete proposal in front of them. The bid was rejected, however, on the grounds that no decision could be taken on the disposal of any major assets. Disappointed and frustrated, I had to sit back and wait till they sorted themselves out.

Some weeks later, perusing *The Financial Times* I was delighted to read that they had done so. At a stormy annual general meeting, the Land & General directors had elected a well-known property specialist and an accountant to the board. Now was the moment to strike. Following a lunch with the chairman, a charming man called Peter Edgington, I arranged to meet the new accountant director, John Skelsey of Booth Anderson & Co. Gently, I put the argument as I saw it. If Penny Brahms won the case of the disputed will, and inherited Land & General, her boy friend's criminal record (he had done time for robbing a Swiss bank) might well cause Sterling to lose their crucial permission to deal in prohibited weapons.

I had done my sums, along with some background research. I knew what I was talking about. I finished by telling Skelsey that I was repeating my offer of £81,000 for the company, but warned him that the offer would remain open for eight days only.

'Eight seconds is all we need, son,' he said, and we shook hands warmly. The Sterling Armament Company was mine.

CHAPTER THREE

A Remarkable Man

Before the advent of the almighty Ford, Sterling had been the largest employer in the Dagenham area. The whole of Sterling Corner at Rainham Road South in Dagenham belonged to the Sterling Cable and Wireless Company, part of which was hived off to become E.M.I., itself now part of the Decca group. Land & General had acquired Sterling in the 1950s following the death of the previous owner, Sir Arnold Braithwaite, M.P.

At one time the Sterling Company was essentially a manufacturer of domestic appliances and diesel engines. Gas mantles, vacuum cleaners and irons were just some of their products. They also made central-heating systems. They even turned out the prototype of a French-designed lorry. However, it was only in their own gun projects that they achieved any degree of world fame.

The first sub-machine gun produced at Sterling was named after George Herbert Lanchester, the gun's designer and the younger brother of the Lanchester of royal car fame. The original Lanchester was almost a carbon copy of the German Schmeisser MP 28 II. It was rushed into production when the British Government belatedly realized the value of what hitherto had been looked down on as gangster guns. This was in 1940, after Dunkirk and the onset of the Battle of Britain, when a German invasion seemed imminent; enemy paratroops were expected to drop out of the sky and capture airfields where their gliders could land, filled with men and towed across from France. The Air Staff urgently required a suitable weapon with which to hose down the invaders. The Schmeisser *Maschinen Pistole* was thought to fit the bill and so an order was hurriedly placed for a British copy.

Despite the haste, the British Schmeisser (as it was first known) was well produced; it met all specifications and functioned satisfactorily. But George Lanchester immediately set about making improvements, chiefly to lighten it.

Meanwhile the Sten gun was being developed by the Royal Small-Arms Factory at Enfield, north London. The name 'Sten' derives from the initials of R. V. Shepherd, in charge of the group, and H. J. Turpin, the designer, with the first two letters of Enfield tacked on. Light in weight and easy to manufacture, the Sten had clear advantages over the Schmeisser copy. Thousands had already been made by the end of 1941, produced both in Britain by BSA (Birmingham Small Arms) and the Royal Ordnance Factory and also in Canada, at the Long Branch Arsenal near Toronto. Contrary to popular belief, Sterling never made the Sten, although there was a complete factory unit given over to making Sten magazines.

Sterling's real success began with one man: George William Patchett. Originally from Nottingham, for a brief period of two days Patchett had been the world's fastest man on two wheels – until somebody else broke his motorcycle record. He went to work for F.N. (Fabrique Nationale) in Herstal, Belgium, which at the time was manufacturing motorcycles, and there he met one of the Browning family who introduced him to the world of guns. From Belgium Patchett went to Czechoslovakia, to work for Janacek (meaning 'Little John') whence came the armour-piercing round for the Allies. He was still there when war broke out, but Churchill himself ordered that Patchett be spirited out of Czechoslovakia with all the Little John drawings on microfilm. While his French wife, again at Churchill's behest, was taken to England via Portugal, Patchett came out through Germany and Holland. He was given a position at Sterling, alongside Lanchester; unfortunately, the two men never got on.

Patchett produced his prototype 9 mm sub-machine gun in 1942. In 1943 it underwent trials against other guns and was deemed to require certain modifications. Patchett pressed on, modifying and adjusting as he thought fit. By 1944 the Army was showing great interest, but the war was nearly over. Not until 1951 was Patchett's design accepted as the best sub-machine gun available. In the final trials at Pendine in Wales, however, there appeared a not insignificant competitor; a very neat and good-looking sub-machine gun from BSA. As Patchett used to tell the story, while the directors of the mighty BSA wined and dined the trials supervisors in the officers' mess, he looked after the sergeants and NCOs in the sergeants' mess — a move that cannot have harmed Sterling's chances, because Patchett's gun was then formally recommended for the Army.

There was one last hitch. When BSA heard they had lost the competition, they asked for a period of grace in which to make some modifications. Patchett was furious; he — rather than Sterling — cried foul. His gun had won, fair and square. There was no point holding final trials if the result was going to be ignored. At last, in September 1953, his gun was adopted by the British Army.

The gun now underwent a change of name. Known throughout its development and trials as the Patchett, it now became known as the Sterling Mark 3 or L2A1. A slightly modified version, the L2A2, was dropped before reaching the production stage but the next model, the Sterling Mark 4 or L2A3, went into production in June 1956. Well over a quarter of a million would be produced in Britain alone, while another 30,000 would be made under licence in Canada (the C.1), with a further quantity in India (the SAF Carbine: probably over a million).

All should have been rosy for both Sterling and Patchett, but then the Ministry of Defence threw their spanner into the works. Sterling, they claimed, was too small a company to be able to fulfil the huge order, and so they set up production at the Royal Ordnance Factory at Fazackerly, Liverpool. Less forgivably, they refused to pay for the use of Patchett's patents.

It was blatant theft. When Patchett and Sterling had recovered from their first stunned disbelief, they sued the Crown through the Ministry of Defence. The M.O.D., like a duchess caught shop-lifting, said in effect, 'Who — *me?*' And when the prosecution attempted to find out the quantity of L2A3s manufactured at Fazackerly, the Official Secrets Act was invoked. It didn't work, and eventually all was revealed: Fazackerly had produced a total of 163,475. But it was a long and bitter fight, although general revulsion at the Government's conduct led to widespread sympathy and support for Patchett and Sterling.

At last, in 1966, they won their case. Patchett was awarded

£116,975, and on that day resigned from Sterling to move to the South of France.

In 1967 the Government adopted the L34A1, or Sterling Patchett Mark 5, the 9 mm silenced version of the Mark 4. It was always Patchett's property and the company made it as a sub-contract.

The fact that the company had called his design by their name had long rankled with Patchett. Not surprisingly, therefore, when I finally settled with him and bought the silenced gun for Sterling, but agreed that it should always carry his name, he was delighted. To me the matter was one of convenience, and saving on adminstrative costs; to him it was a matter of due recognition.

I met George Patchett several times. He was a remarkable person. Tall, very fit, even in his seventies he would either swim every day or ski, depending on where he was. His house in Cannes was filled with inventions and gadgets. At the end of the war he had gone to the directors of Sterling with an idea, a small electric motor in a housing with a drill chuck. The Sterling employees referred to it as the 'pig', but history does not relate whether this was because of its shape or because they felt some aversion to the prospect of having to tool it up. The prospect never became a reality, however. The directors scoffed at Patchett's idea. A power tool for the handyman? What an idea! As if the British working man would be in the frame of mind to go home after his hard day's toil and continue to labour in his own back yard! But if Patchett's idea had been developed, Sterling would have been twenty years ahead of Wolf, Black & Decker and Bosch. It was the same patronizing attitude as shown by those who had planned the Dagenham housing estates, back in the days when Ford moved into the area: obviously the British working man would never be able to afford a car, so there was no need to make the streets wide or to build garages.

The last time I saw George he was as bouncy and well as always. He insisted on showing me elaborate architectural drawings that he had completed for the Patchett family mausoleum, where he and everyone else in the family would find a last resting place. That was in March 1978. Less than a month later he was dead.

CHAPTER FOUR

Settling In

I now had myself a gun factory. There was work to do, but first I had to assess more fully what state the place was in. To help me in my task I had invaluable support from two men in particular. The first was a retired major of Marines (equivalent to a lieutenant-colonel in Army terms), Bernard Beavan Keen. At one time the senior Marine on HMS *Belfast*, he looked like the archetypal major, with his small moustache and brown trilby. I once mentioned that my father-in-law never trusted a man who wore a hat when driving, and Major Keen went bare-headed from thenceforth. He was an expert in military weapons, having specialized in this field while in the Service.

The other man was David Howroyd. A big man, but quiet, calm and precise, he had been with Sterling all his working life, starting as a toolmaker, except for his wartime service as an airframe fitter in the R.A.F. He had been groomed for the job of works director, and when the then works director − also a director of Land & General − took the opportunity to retire, David was well able to fill his shoes. He had actually been sacked by George Patchett, not once but twice, for changing existing drawings in order to achieve certain small but significant improvements in the gun's performance. On both occasions Patchett apologized and had him reinstated. David was always working to extend the gun's accuracy, making improvements to the bolt and miniscule alterations to the chamber of the barrel. But tact was not one of his strengths. We had become aware that feed problems could occur with certain ammunition produced by the Finnish company Lapua, who used some peculiar brass specification in their 9 mm cases; and when the

Finnish authorities purchased two sub-machine guns for testing purposes, David wrote telling them expressly that Lapua ammunition should not be used, and why.

It was David's advice I sought when considering what to do with one of the company's assets: a de Havilland Dragon Rapide. It had no engines and was packed in elaborate teak crates. David, the ex-airframe fitter, was disparaging. It would never fly again, he said, so I sold it for the value of the crates. But I discovered years later that the aircraft had been restored and is now an all-time classic, worth thousands of pounds.

In fact, the money from the sale of the crates was a useful boost to our finances at the time. When the Sterling site at Dagenham was redeveloped, the factory had been obliged to move out to Chadwell Heath, a few miles to the north. Now Russell Newbury, the diesel engine manufacturer that had also been under Land & General ownership, found suitable accommodation back on the original Sterling Corner site, and, eager to avoid a penal rent arrangement with Brixton Estates Ltd, we unanimously decided to return 'home' as quickly as possible. Ironically we were now in what had been the Sten magazine factory.

After the actual removals, the main expenditure was to be in the building of a bond (a secure place in which to store sub-machine guns) and offices, and so, in order to save money, we built the latter ourselves. It took just one week-end, thanks to our very own Stud Fixing Tool. Made by the company, this had been devised as a piece of equipment for use by sappers, for example when they wanted to mine a bridge in a hurry. It was a kind of super Hilti nail gun, which could also be used as a fourteen-shot repeating firearm, and hence needed a full firearms licence. It had proved a commercial failure, as under the laws of Proof for gun barrels, the fourteen-shot magazine had been deemed to carry fourteen barrels, and so each gun had to be proof-fired fourteen times. The old company had therefore sold it off to a third party, but for our purposes it was invaluable.

The removals complete and construction under way, I tried to concentrate on the company's commercial position. Already well aware that sales were static, I was convinced this was because of some failing in company policy rather than in the product. One factor stood out above all. Back in the early 1960s the company had signed an agreement with the Indian Government, allowing them to build the Sterling under licence for their own armed forces. Part of the deal was that India should take 50,000 Sterlings made by the company, to be paid for by the British Government under an Aid to India contract. Then, in 1965, war broke out between India and Pakistan. Not wishing to take sides, the British Government cancelled the export licence. Sterling's contract, however, had been with the Foreign and Commonwealth Office, and the company enforced the contract to the full. The 50,000 Sterlings went into the stores at Donnington in Shropshire, gradually being sold off by Her Majesty's Government at their 1961 manufactured price – in competition, of course, with anything that the company produced subsequently.

Perhaps I should explain that the Sterlings did not go into service with the British Army because there were certain differences between the L2A3, the Army version, and the Mark 4 Sterling. The L2A3 has a reinforcing plate in the butt frame, a different rear-sight, a different chamber in the barrel (which will not accept such a general range of 9 mm Parabellum ammunition) and it lacks the Sterling's crackle-finish black paint. Also, the L2A3 used a two-part magazine, as made by Rolls Razor, Mettoy and Fazackerly, whereas the Mark 4 used the company's own stronger four-part box magazine.

When I came on the scene, there were still about 10,000 of these 'old' Sterlings left in the stores at Donnington. I applied to the Government to buy them back. But the Government would not play ball; it had been decided that the remaining stock of guns would be cannibalized for spares. This was good news and bad news. The bad news was that the company had been hoping to win a large order to manufacture spares for the M.O.D. and our prospective order would now shrink, although, as they could not use the barrels, they would still have to ask Sterling to make the L2A3-pattern barrels afresh. The good news was that the company was now master of its own destiny, and could make and sell Sterlings profitably.

I had already effectively doubled the selling price of the Mark 4. Now, obviously, we had to win some orders.

It was hard to know where to begin. The company received a

constant trickle of small orders and enquiries from various forces around the world, but, on the grounds of economy, Major Keen had been prevented from travelling abroad to follow these up. I understood the reasoning, although it seemed most likely that our future depended on foreign sales, and in substantial quantities.

Meanwhile I changed the prefix to the serial number on all Sterling guns. It had been KR (the initials of a former managing director, Kenton Redgrave). It now became SI, in tribute to my wife, Sisi − but also because the letters SI are infinitely quicker to engrave on a pantograph engraving machine.

Another early concern was to sort out the Australian Government. Evidently dissatisfied with their own sub-machine gun, a very odd-looking affair with the magazine on top of the weapon, they had decided to adopt the Sterling magazine, partly on its own merits, but partly also to have commonality with the British. They had asked Sterling for a licence on the magazine and had been quoted a huge amount. At this they told Sterling to take two fingers (one, in American parlance); they were going ahead with the manufacture and if Sterling did not like it they could sue the Commonwealth of Australia in Australia. When I bought Sterling I could see no point in pursuing this expensive case, for little or no return, and called the whole thing off. I then made myself known to the Australian High Commission in Aldwych, London. They ended up buying a quantity of Mark 5s, and we became firm friends. In fact, during my time at Sterling I regularly dropped in on a Friday afternoon so that they could ply me with Australian lager.

Gradually the orders were increasing. Perhaps doubling the price of the Mark 4 had produced the desired effect; or perhaps it was just luck. Major Keen had been talking to the Libyan Government, whose armed forces were run along British Army lines; they already had some 5,000 Sterlings and now it transpired that they were so pleased with them they wanted to order 10,000 more. The real coup was that Major Keen secured a 50% deposit for the whole amount, although this had to be guaranteed through the Libyans' bank in London, Crédit Lyonnais at South Kensington. The British authorities were happy to grant an export licence and the first shipment of guns was sent, along with a huge overbalance of magazines.

The company now had resources. Not only could we finance the odd jaunt overseas to round up some more orders, we could even think about broadening our range of products.

I'd been asking Major Keen some fairly inane questions about guns – he was very patient with me – and generally trying to mug up on the subject. My wife had presented me with a copy of *Smith's Small Arms of the World*. I had pored over all the company's old correspondence. The idea formed in my mind that we needed another gun to make, ideally one that would sell on the civilian as well as the military markets.

In the early '60s the company had made an approach to the Colt Firearms Company in Hartford, Connecticut, to take a licence on the 5.56 mm M-16 rifle. This rifle had been designed by a team headed up by Eugene Stoner, who was working for Armalite Inc. of Costa Mesa, California. Their designation for the rifle was AR-15, but it changed its name when the American Government adopted it. I was curious to learn that the British M.O.D. had bought 5,000 AR-15s for the forces in Borneo, during the confrontation with Indonesia. Equally interesting was the discussion that ensued over the instability of the American 5.56 mm round, and how it tumbled and caused explosive wounds. It was all a question of distance. Some Royal Marines who had used the AR-15 in Borneo described how they had shot at a goat – for food, presumably – and the animal just carried on grazing. The bullet had passed straight through.

From Colt's point of view, Sterling would have been a useful ally in persuading Britain and the Commonwealth to take the rifle, perhaps even other European members of Nato. The American Government had been keen to step up production, because of the Vietnam War – so keen, in fact, that it paid $4.5 million to Colt to let Harrington and Richardson and the Hydramatic Division of General Motors produce the gun under licence (the Americans were distinctly better behaved than our own dear Government). But, to the despair of Major Robert Turp, Beavan Keen's predecessor at Sterling, the U.S. Government prevented the export of even sample guns. Politically, perhaps, it seemed inadvisable to share production with a foreign company, especially when there were plenty of competent indigenous producers. Or possibly there were political complications on this side of the Atlantic, with Harold Wilson and the Labour Government so adamant that Britain should have nothing to do with the Vietnam War; there might certainly have been questions over whether British export licences would be granted. On a personal note, though, I would never have been able to buy Sterling if the deal had gone through.

While frustrating at the time, the episode seemed to have planted a seed at Sterling. The 5.56 mm assault rifle was going into service; more than that, cut-down versions were already being considered as replacements for the sub-machine gun. We decided, now, to commission our own design of 5.56 mm rifle. We presented Frank Waters, Sterling's chief designer, with our requirements and gave him the go-ahead. In the meantime, flying a kite, I wrote to Armalite in California. They had the products and we had the production capacity; I was sure we could do business.

Before buying Sterling I had been introduced to a gunsmith called Bob Jennings. I met him in Jules Bar in Jermyn Street, just off Piccadilly; apparently it used to be a favourite haunt of arms dealers. Benign, friendly and highly knowledgeable, he had given me some good advice over Sterling, warning of possible pitfalls and indicating where the company had gone wrong in the past. He and Beavan Keen were friends; they both lived in Fareham where Bob had a shop (Jennings & Groves, as it was then; now Jennings & Patterson). He was a small-arms and special weapons expert, and was currently making specials in the extensive and very well-equipped factory area behind the sleepy facade of his gun shop. Visiting him there reminded me of the Belgian specialist gunmaker in Frederick Forsyth's book, *The Day of the Jackal*. To my astonishment I learnt that Bob had been in the Royal Navy for 18 years. Even more astonishing, he had been to sea for less than a year of that time. His specialist skills were clearly more useful on land.

Bob had formed an association with two Scots, David Wilson, a recently retired brigadier from the illustrious Argyll and Sutherland Highlanders, and Hugh McWhinnie. Hugh started the Second World War as a corporal in the Black Watch and ended his career as full colonel in the American Army: as some wag put it, an exercise in demotion. Hugh, who retained his Scots economy of words, now represented the Brazilian vehicle manufacturer, Engesa, and an American manufacturer of night-vision systems, Asferonics Inc. of Leesburg, Virginia. The three of them together had identified a role for a night weapon-sight. (This was before Pilkington, Rank or English Electric entered the field.)

Infra-red systems had been around for some time, but this scheme was totally new. Its enormous advantage was that, unlike infra-red, it could not be detected. As the Soviets were training whole divisions of the Red Army to live and fight at night, the West would clearly need to develop appropriate technology such as image intensifiers.

Bob soon had me fascinated with talk of the night-vision system; his part in it was to adapt the viewer into a sight, with all the inherent problems of graticules, mounts and interfacing the mounts between different weapons. It was, he said, particularly effective and impressive on a sub-machine gun that was properly silenced — one like the Mark 5 Sterling Patchett silenced gun, or L34A1.

The seventy-two holes drilled within the rifling of the Sterling's barrel bleed off enough gas to slow the bullet to just supersonic speed, thus preventing the 'crack'. With a gas diffuser tube and silencer that contained no perishable rubber parts, or anything that would otherwise need replacement, it fired absolutely standard 9 mm Parabellum ammunition with no more noise than an electric typewriter — ninety-two decibels — and was quite unrecognizable as a firearm. It was, I knew, a formidable weapon, and remarkably accurate. Together with the night-vision system, it would certainly be unique.

A real door-opener.

Bob Jennings and I decided to make a joint sales tour of the Far East.

CHAPTER FIVE

The Orient

Beavan Keen made all the arrangements for our Far East trip through Sterling's existing agents, then gave me a crash course in how to show the Sterling off to best effect. Near Fareham, Bob Jennings had the use of an old quarry, dotted around with Figure 11 targets, the crouching oriental soldier, and I went down there one afternoon for a course of instruction.

Beavan Keen began by teaching me a few tricks for demonstrating the Sterling, like firing with the butt resting on the chin. If the gun is pushed against the chin it cannot kick, as the power of the recoil is not very great. He also taught me to lean forward slightly when firing in the fully automatic mode. He particularly impressed me by holding the gun in the flat palm of his hand, then firing it fully automatic to show that the gun did not climb. His little insurance policy was the fact that the bayonet boss was well gripped between two fingers!

As evening fell it was time for me to try my hand with the night-vision sights. First I was given a Mark 4 Sterling fitted with a Singlepoint sight. Five inches long, this is used with both eyes open, and a light-reflected red dot shows on the target. In quick semi-automatic fire, as a comparative novice I scored a bull on eighteen out of eighteen targets.

I already knew a bit about the Singlepoint. Bob Jennings had been managing director of Singlepoint UK before resigning to concentrate on his own projects. Optics is a particularly complicated area and this was a very clever invention, but it never made a hit in the military field. Basically, the reason for this unjustified lack of success was that it was always sold as 'the Singlepoint sight'. It was not a sight; it was a quick-aiming device. Used as a sight it could be inaccurate if the firer took too long over the aim, because the eyes might refocus before he actually fired his shot. In the quick aim, however, it is absolutely superb. Some soldiers bought it privately and fitted it to their weapons in Northern Ireland, until the M.O.D. forbade them to do so following tests conducted under sight conditions.

By now it was night, cloudy, moonless and totally dark. I was handed the Mark 5 with the new image-intensifier sight, the Scotos designed by Bob Jennings and his associates and made by Asferonics. I pressed my eye into the rubber egg-cup of the eye-piece. I could see everything as clearly as if in broad daylight; the only difference was that the image appeared in shades of bright green. Again, bulls on all eighteen targets. What a gadget for taking out sentries!

Beavan Keen saw us off at Heathrow airport in case we had any problems relating to the goods. These included two Mark 4s, two Mark 5s, two Scotos sights and mounts for various other weapons so that sights and guns would not have to be continually zeroed in, and a Scotos hand-held viewer. Firearms regulations then were not quite so dire as they are today, but we still had to have all our documentation in order. By chance, the duty officer on Thai International was sporting a Royal Marines tie, and Beavan Keen soon got him talking. The result was that Bob and I were upgraded to first class. It was a good omen for the trip.

The flight was superb and early the next morning we landed at Bangkok. Emerging into the clammy heat we were taken to our hotel, the Siam Intercontinental, for a rest and a freshen-up. Sterling's head agent in the area, covering several countries, was Maclaine Watson in Singapore, where our affairs were handled by Geoffrey Millington, a retired R.A.F. air commodore. Millington had flown into Bangkok and would meet us later, but the agent's representatives in Thailand − part of an American-owned organization, Siam Teltech − had sent a very worldly Chinese called Sidh to smooth our path at the Airport. Sidh arranged for the hardware to be kept in custody with the airport police, as he had planned a demonstration for the following day at the nearby Thai Air Force base.

That first afternoon, although we managed to avoid the assorted bath-houses and massage parlours, we did our cultural bit by touring Buddhist temples, one after another, until we were sick of the sight of them. In the evening Sidh had arranged dinner in a Chinese restaurant, where Geoffrey Millington joined the party. A bevy of oriental beauties flocked in, sat themselves between us and tried to feed us. They dabbed our mouths with napkins and made it plain they had been instructed to cater for our every need. And sure enough, towards the end of the meal, a little hand started to edge up and curl itself around the inside of my thigh. I was saved from a beautiful fate by the fact that we had to get up early the next morning, to battle our way through the Bangkok traffic and prepare for the demonstration. As we left the restaurant we were met by yet more beauties, all asking if we wanted 'a good time'. One of them, more anxious than the rest for business, lifted her skirt: she was wearing nothing underneath, and betrayed the fact that she was a he. There was much to learn about the East.

The next day we made our way to the air base to prepare for our demonstration. For me it was a slightly nervous time, but being with an expert like Bob Jennings I knew I could not go far wrong. Besides, if any immediate decision needed to be made, I had to be on the spot.

We had informed the British Embassy of our demonstration, and the Defence Attaché came to assist, a serving Brigade of Guards colonel. Then at the appointed time our audience arrived: generals and admirals and representatives of all the services. To our satisfaction, the night-vision system and the silent gun attracted close interest. The gun was taken out to be used on an open-air range, so that its silenced effect should not be marred by the thud of bullets hitting the end of the range indoors. A Thai soldier provided conclusive proof of the gun's ability; after firing a standard Uzi he was given the Mark 4 Sterling – and, holding it for the first time in his life, he achieved a quite astonishing improvement in his grouping.

It puzzled me that the Thais should have adopted the Uzi when the Malays, with similar terrain, had had such success with the Sterling. Bob warned me to prepare myself for a series of disappointments. In the small-arms world, he said, the right decision is often compromised by politics, economics or the philosophy of straight corruption. Sterling had never really tried to sell the gun to the Thais and the Defence Attaché at the time was probably involved in other things; in other words, a good market had been lost by default.

Still on the subject of the Uzi, Bob said it had been adopted in many countries just because the Israelis had shouted louder than anyone else. Politics, he said, had boosted the Uzi. For himself, he liked the compact feel to it and the magazine that fitted through the pistol grip, although he preferred the Austrian Steyr MP i 69, which was similar. The Sterling is two pounds lighter than the Uzi, much more accurate and also more reliable in mud and sand. Also, the Uzi cannot be silenced effectively, on account of its wrap-around bolt construction, and it cannot accept a curved magazine. (The sides of the 9 mm Parabellum round are not parallel. If laid down side by side, the rounds form a natural curve which is why the Sterling magazine is curved.) The Sterling, moreover, had won outright a competition for adoption by West Germany's Bundeswehr. The General Staff decision to adopt it was later overturned by the Defence Minister, Franz Josef Strauss, who discovered that the cost of adopting the Uzi could be offset against West German war reparations. In those days Israel's military industries were embryonic, and so the Uzi was made under licence by FN (Fabrique Nationale) in Belgium, the largest military small-arms manufacturer in the world, whose own standing naturally enhanced the product's chances on international markets (except in the Arab nations, of course).

By the time we left Bangkok, a day and a half later, I was beginning to feel more confident. Only time would tell whether the orders would come in, but we had won considerable good will among the Thais and made personal contact with several useful people. But now we were off to Malaysia.

Our agent in Malaysia was Haji Mat Jan bin Haji Wok, or Mat Jan for short. He had been the Force Armament Officer in the Royal Malaysian Police. A paramilitary field force, British-styled and considerably larger numerically than the army, the Police Force was a huge customer of Sterling's, sending in regular orders for both guns and spares. Mat was gentle, charming, religious, and always well dressed. At first I felt a little inhibited by him, and was glad to have Bob with me in case I said anything foolish, but in time we became very close friends.

Malaysia had won independence from Britain only a decade or so earlier, and there were certain areas where the Malays remained rather sensitive. The British, I learnt, might have left the legacy of a good judicial system and fine administration, but they were regarded as insufferably arrogant, pompous and offensive. Obviously there were exceptions, but the overall impression left behind by the British in Malaysia was one of overweening conceit. What's more, I still see this arrogance in the attitude of some Brits when dealing with foreigners today. Probably the only people who have got used to it, and know how to snub it without the Brits realizing, are the Americans – themselves once subject to colonial rule.

Bob had spent some time in Malaya when he was in the Navy. He told me of the tensions between Malays and Chinese, and how the Malaysian Government had developed their Bumiputra ('Sons of the Soil') policy to make sure that the Chinese did not swamp Malayan enterprise. He also recounted a few of his exploits during the Emergency. Trained in jungle warfare, he was sent off to catch 'C.T.s' (Communist Terrorists) whom he had to identify from photographs. Together with a Malay assistant and a Dayak tracker, he stalked C.T.s through the jungle and either shot or knifed them to death. In order to confirm each kill, his party had to remove the head with a panga and then take it back to base for identification. The main problem was getting the severed heads back to base, in hessian sacks, before the smell became overpowering; in that jungle heat, putrefaction was rapid. Bob was proud of his exploits; he assured me that it was not too often that they got the wrong head.

Mat was well in with the police, of course, and had some interesting agencies. The army was another matter; there was a rivalry between police and army and he did not like visiting them. At the time, there was a move to equip the army with 5.56 mm rifles, and sizable orders had already gone to Italy (5,000 Beretta M-70s), Germany (5,000 Heckler & Koch HK-33s) and the USA (5,000 Colt M-16s). In fact the Heckler & Koch rifle with its delayed blow-back system had won the trials, and some 50,000 had gone into service after being locally assembled; but they had just been rejected, and the whole 5.56 mm-calibre rifle competition was again open. The army was very keen to see what Sterling could produce, so Bob and I naturally made every effort to encourage their interest. In the end, however, when Singapore had bought a licence and set up their own manufacture at Chartered Industries, the Malaysians did adopt the same M-16 and set up local assembly – then still later dropped it in favour of the Austrian AUG. Such a variable procurement policy must have been a nightmare for the armourers, having to keep up to date with different service manuals and a multiplicity of spare parts. Oddly, the Malaysian Armed Forces had an equally unaccountable assortment of vehicles. The only explanation seems to be that the Malaysians wanted to keep 'current benefactors' on their toes.

Before leaving Kuala Lumpur, Bob and I were wined and dined by Mat Jan and his chairman in the restaurant at the top of the new Hilton. Again, some ladies were brought along for company; it was as if we were being tested (I was always conscious of the risk of being blackmailed). Had we not been on business, things might have been different. As it was, I had the greatest difficulty in shaking off the delectable Eurasian laid on for my personal benefit.

In Singapore we had a chance to relax a bit. We stayed at the Goodwood Park, which before the First World War had been the German Embassy. Although Geoffrey Millington lived in Singapore, he was not our agent there; but in the past I had done some deals with a young Chinese businessman called Goh ee Keng and he was keen to act for us. Slight and good-looking, with an almost Italian air about him, Goh impressed us with his contacts in the police and prison service, and in Singapore Customs. Thanks to him, we spent a most interesting evening aboard a Customs launch, watching the mass of shipping through the night-vision viewer. The automatic brightness control, a unique feature of our Scotos 'scopes, meant that they were not blinded even if a bright light was shone directly at them; they merely adjusted themselves to compensate. The Customs people were very enthusiastic. Their main interest in the equipment was to watch for drug trafficking.

Each time we gave a demonstration our wares were escorted by the Singapore Government's answer to Burns in the USA and Britain, a specialist security firm called Cisco whose guards toted Sterlings wherever they went. Apart from that, my only noteworthy memory of that stay in Singapore is of a visit to Bugis Street. Long since demolished, like so much else in that modern island metropolis, Bugis Street came to life at night when it was frequented by transvestites, one more beautiful than another. They appeared to be touting for business, so I can only assume they were homosexuals (gays had not been invented then). We bought some of them drinks and listened to their stories. They came from all walks of life, all colours and creeds. Some were saving up for 'the operation'; others had had it. Beautiful, sad and puzzling people, I couldn't help contrasting them with some of the European women we saw the following day, when Geoffrey Millington took us as his guests to the Tanglin Club for Sunday lunch. This was the top haven for expatriate residents in Singapore − the tradition was to have a curry lunch every Sunday − and it was filled with chattering groups of wives and widows, all seeming very large and coarse and loud by comparison with the elegant enigmas of the night before.

Our next destination was Jakarta, a vast, dirty, ugly city, teeming with people. Although formerly called Batavia and capital of the Dutch East Indies, nothing there remains of Holland except the letters NV after a company name. Our Indonesian agents, of Chinese origin, were friendly with Leo Lopulisa, the top general of the Special Forces. These boys had seen active service in Vietnam and they loved the demonstration. We nearly started off on the wrong foot, though. As usual, preparing for the demonstration we'd set up our Figure 11 targets around the range, then realized too late that the crouching oriental soldier was less than tactful in the circumstances. But, to our surprise, the Indonesians merely burst out laughing; then all was explained when one of our guests remarked, 'Obviously *you* don't like the Japanese either!'

They all handled the weapons very well, but there was no chance of selling them the Mark 4, since the military factory at Bandung was already turning out the Beretta Model 12 sub-machine gun for the TNI (Indonesian Army). A year or two later when I visited the small-arms factory at Bandung − a huge establishment, put up by Fritz Werner and bigger than Smith & Wesson − I was astounded to find that its sole product line consisted of belt buckles. The Germans, Italians and their agents must have been well rewarded for this white elephant.

Indonesia had a reputation for being rife with 'corruption', as we in the West would call it. I knew for a fact that army officers were very lowly paid, yet they could afford cars, houses, servants and all the other trappings of a comfortable life — which indicated that 'skimming' was a widespread and recognized perk. But, in its defence, such a country does not have a civil service complete with procurement executives engaged in a charade of sea-green incorruptibility. Agent and officer might collude over some item of new equipment, but if ever that equipment was faulty they would be in dire trouble, and neither would be likely to have another bite at the cherry.

Bob and I had an unexpected frisson in Jakarta. He met somebody in the bar of the Hotel Indonesia who asked him if he would be interested in buying diamonds . . . To cut a long story short, we were taken to a private house and shown some enormous blue diamonds from Kalimantan. They were for sale at a tenth of the price we would have had to pay in Amsterdam — so we were told. But neither of us knew a thing about diamonds. Besides, even a 90% discount could not persuade us to forget the warnings we'd had that this might be a police trap. I've never seen any diamonds since of comparable size.

Next on our itinerary were the Philippines: back to Geoffrey Millington's province. The agent here was a man called Joe Larcina. Joe had been a successful trader in Shanghai and, possessed of a neutral Spanish passport, had stayed there throughout the Japanese occupation. In 1950 he moved to Saigon and later to Manila where he married a Filipino girl and had a family. He told us that when Mao and the Red Chinese Army chased out the Kuomintang, the Chinese nationalist government under Chiang Kai-shek, the officers spoke Japanese; they were rumoured to be the remnants of an Imperial Army that had mysteriously disappeared during the war.

The Secretary General of Defense for the Philippines, Manuel Q. Salientes, was a friend of Joe's — and somewhat to my astonishment I found that he even had an office within Joe's suite. But again, such open acceptance of the realities of life had its advantages; at least everyone knew where they were. A distinguished-looking man with receding hairline and bushy 'bugger grips', Salientes told us that he had heard our stuff was good and that we could expect an order worth one million pounds. I relished a moment of triumph, but it was fleeting. I had actually seen the document of contract between Colt and the Elisco Tool & Die Corporation for the manufacture of the M-16 rifle in the Philippines: the figures were astronomic, for obvious reasons. And then Salientes added that there was one small condition. Imelda Marcos often went to London on a private basis and she wanted to be able to drop in − unofficially, of course − on the Queen. If I could arrange that, Salientes would see I got my order. As a matter of interest, when I returned to London I called a friend in the Foreign Office. The answer came back six weeks later: a definite NO!

That afternoon we held our demonstration as planned, more for goodwill purposes than because we expected results. On the way there, escorted by Colonel Ernesto Luis, we passed through the army camp and saw two soldiers taking an outside shower. Each had the most enormous pizzle. Bob and I started laughing, and the Colonel asked why. Then, following our glance, he snorted too. 'Oh I see,' he said. 'As Filipinos go they are a little underdeveloped. But let's put it down to the cold weather we're having.'

There was not much time before we left the Philippines, but I wanted to track down someone called Sotero Tambongco. Sterling had received a number of orders from him, in lots of 50 sub-machine guns at a time, each order accompanied by a cheque, traveller's cheque, dollar bills or anything negotiable. But suddenly his orders had stopped. It was about the time that Ferdinand Marcos started flexing his strong-arm rule. Now was my chance to find out what had happened. I went to Tambongco's address in Makati, but there was no sign of anyone there. I went to the neighbours to see if they knew where he was, but they looked frightened. They knew nothing, they insisted, and the door was slammed in my face. It was very unsatisfactory, but I had to leave the matter like that − though possibly it was just as well.

Now we were off to Hong Kong, though just by way of a rest. The guns were left at Kai Tak airport but we gave a night demonstration to the Hong Kong Police. They already had plenty of Sterlings and claimed they could not afford any more. This was at the height of the corruption scandal; the Investigating Council Against Corruption had just been appointed (commonly referred to by its initials, which some people said stood for 'Interference with Chinese Ancient Customs' or 'I Can't Accept Cheques'). We dared not offer a sweetener!

My wife flew out to join us in Hong Kong, and, coincidentally, so did our neighbours. There were also several old school and university friends around. We all stayed in the Mandarin, which was very comfortable and central, and had a thoroughly good time.

From Hong Kong Bob and I planned to fly to Taiwan, but shortly before we were due to leave we had a visit from a British civil servant. He made it plain that we were expected to cancel our trip, or at the very least to leave any British weaponry behind. No reason was given. Furthermore, his manner was rude and rather overbearing. We told him that we had made a commitment to Maclaine Watson's agent in T'ai-pei and we were going to honour it. We would not take the Sterlings, but we were going to show the American night-vision equipment. Muttering threats that the Embassy would not be able to help us if we ran into trouble, and warning us not to expect any more help from British defence officials, the man left. When we had calmed down, Bob and I had a moment's reflection. The man had failed to explain why we should do what he wanted; he had not even said who had sent him to deliver this message. We did not feel we had any justification for letting down Tommy Chao or Asferonics by not showing the equipment.

So we went to Taiwan. It was a short but entirely uneventful stay. After a few more days in Hong Kong, we finally tore ourselves away from the hectic social round to fly west to Nepal. Here in the mountain kingdom there is a strong link with the British Army, and many Sterlings were in evidence. There is enormous pride among the Gurkhas who have served in British Army regiments. Other Gurkha regiments are in service with the Indian Army, and Lee Kwan Yew, the then prime minister of Singapore, had a Gurkha bodyguard. Our own agent was a sophisticated Gurkha called Rama Shrestha, who now lives in Fort Worth, Texas.

We gave several demonstrations to very appreciative audiences in Nepal, including the Police Force. They immediately ordered six hand-held Scotos night-viewing devices − very expensive items for such an impoverished country to pay for, but we assumed that their need warranted the expense. Indeed, we heard that there was some sort of unrest in central Nepal and the authorities did not want us venturing anywhere near it. But we were very happy in the Soaltee Oberoi Hotel, just on the edge of Kathmandu, where Freddy the barman, an Englishman who had been there for 20 years, mixed the most amazing port-and-cream cocktail: he called it a Pink Pearl. It was quite delicious.

I have two other memories of Kathmandu. One was the sight of a woman actually giving birth in the street. The other was the erotic carvings on the temples, of all places: the most amazing array, wonderful to contemplate but impossible to describe, except to say that the carvings showed every permutation of who could do what to whom. The only Western equivalent to this variety and spectacle is Lord Weymouth's murals at Longleat in Wiltshire.

While in Nepal we took the opportunity to visit Tiger Tops, a hotel in a game reserve on the Indian border. Jim Edwards, who owns Tiger Tops, had become involved in the attempts to breed up the tiger, and apparently with some success. Tigers in this area had become nearly extinct, but now it seems there is some hope for them. Flying down from Kathmandu to the camp, we were hosted by James Stewart's daughter; she looked and spoke exactly like her actor father. The game reserve was quite unlike any African game park. It was forested in parts, and the plains were covered in dense, tall grass, easily eight or ten feet high, so that the only way to see anything was from the back of an elephant. It was a slow way of getting around the reserve but very pleasant and, especially for the wildlife enthusiasts, well worth the experience.

Our last stop was India. We did not have an agent here, but many retired Indian generals expressed the wish to represent Sterling. The Sterling gun was made under licence in an arsenal in Jabalpur, and I hoped to sell them a manufacturing licence for the Mark 5 too. The Indian Army was eager for a demonstration but we ran into problems with our paperwork. Even a brigadier-general failed to talk Customs into letting our guns through without the necessary papers. My wife, who had flown into New Delhi with us, had also had a spot of trouble on her arrival. It was noticed that her passport indicated she had been born in South Africa; she was made to wait at the back of the queue until everyone else had been processed. Only then was she let through.

India is an extremely important market, and the Defence Attaché in the High Commission was a general, no less. Major-General

Richardson, resplendent in Khaki uniform, red flashes and tabs, and oak leaves, took Bob and me into those awe-inspiring Government buildings designed by Lutyens and now housing the Indian Ministry of Defence. But behind the grand façade, those magnificent buildings were full of dingy offices and long dreary corridors cluttered with motor scooters and bundles of papers tied up with faded red tape in true Dickensian fashion. However, the General stepped out briskly with us in tow. A sonorous 'Good morning' here, a smart salute there, and he had all the Indians snapping to attention. They loved a real British general, and Richardson certainly knew how to ham it up. That evening he hosted a dinner party for us, and some of the relevant Indian generals were invited. Richardson's staff were Mahrattas, dressed in dark blue with scarlet turbans secured by Royal Artillery cap badges. In my book at least, he scored eleven out of ten for presentation.

We were staying at the Imperial Hotel in Jan Path, where the assassination of Gandhi was filmed; it was an old traditional hotel, not yet touched by the stereotyped ideas of American hotels, and all the more enjoyable for that. But my wife was unhappy about all the poverty and wretchedness she'd seen; although her family boasted soldiers and administrators in India, going back for generations, she could not stand it for long. We decided to spend our last afternoon together on a visit to Delhi's Red Fort, and arrived to find President Numeiry of the Sudan giving an address to the Indian people. There were few people around to listen to him, and those who were there did not understand one word of what he was saying. However, it was good to sit in the early evening sunshine and watch the amazing bird life that abounds even in the middle of Delhi. That night my wife flew back to England.

Bob and I would not be far behind her. After completing our business we found ourselves caught in Delhi over a national holiday, and decided to spend one last day sightseeing. We hired a taxi − they all looked like 1950s Morris Oxfords, made by the Hindustan Motor Company − and set off for Agra, some 120 miles away, to see the Taj Mahal. On the way our driver managed to hit a mongoose and a cyclist, but it was what he (just) missed that was so terrifying. Even 20 years ago the Taj Mahal was swarming with tourists, but it really is one of the wonders of the world, and well worth the agony of getting there.

In the hotel we had run into Walter Clode, an urbane former Guards officer and now the owner of Westley Richards, the finest of the Birmingham shotgun and rifle makers. Walter used to tour India buying up old English sporting guns and armouries, in the same way that old Rolls-Royces were collected. However, guns too seemed to have run out, so Walter had turned his attention to jewelled daggers and any other collectable items he could lay his hands on.

I suppose I had picked up a few souvenirs of my own, but they were trinkets compared with the memories I was taking home. India, with its contrasts and colour, the Taj Mahal and bodies being disposed of by the birds along the river banks. Nepal and those erotic carvings. Thailand, the Philippines, Indonesia. . . And, of course, all that I had learnt from Bob, my expert colleague and companion, about guns, people and places. But my mind was buzzing, reverberating with all the sights and sounds and impressions. I was glad to be going home.

CHAPTER SIX

Courting a Partner

Whether or not the Far East trip had been a success was not immediately apparent. As yet we had no firm orders, but Bob and I were both convinced we had made a substantial impact in certain quarters. And, less obvious but arguably just as important, we had increased goodwill by taking the trouble to make personal contact.

Back in London I was particularly interested to learn that George Sullivan of Armalite Inc. had been in touch. He had received my letter and, since he was coming to London shortly on other business, suggested we should meet. Sullivan, a patent attorney with bottle-top spectacles, had co-founded Armalite with Chuck Dorchester, originally to develop sporting guns. It was really a research and development organization, although at times they swung into production of various items in their range. It was a long and impressive range of products, including the AR-5 and the .22" Hornet Survival Rifle (accepted by the USAF as the MA-1), whose bolt, barrel, trigger, receiver and magazine, when disassembled, could all be packed into the plastic butt. The civilian version, the AR-7, which was sold to Charter Arms and became known as the Explorer, featured in one of the James Bond films. Another highlight of the Armalite list was the AR-10, developed by Eugene Stoner, their Chief Engineer. This was a 7.62 mm automatic rifle, light and comfortable to fire although it had a lot of recoil. Commercially it was never a hit, unlike its direct descendant the AR-15 (M-16), which was Armalite's most successful design ever, still being produced by Colt, Chartered Industries in Singapore, Elisco Tool & Die in the Philippines, and in South Korea.

Sullivan had done well from the M-16 royalties and the company had then gone on to develop a more conventional 5.56 mm military rifle, which would be cheap and simple to produce: the AR-180. Armalite made the first production run, but the manufacture had been set up at the Howa Machinery Company of Nagoya, in Japan, and Armalite then relied upon Howa to supply approximately 7,000 AR-180s annually for the American civilian market. It was a semi-automatic version of the AR-18 and was specifically designed so that conversion back to full automatic capability would be well nigh impossible. Unfortunately for both Armalite and Howa, a number of the rifles somehow reached the Irish Republican Army in Northern Ireland, and the Japanese Government – always sensitive to charges of militarism – thereafter imposed a total ban on their export. Now Armalite were keen to find a partner, a manufacturer to replace Howa.

When George Sullivan arrived, I met him and his wife Jean at the London Hilton where they were staying, and it was agreed that we should examine further the possibility of collaboration.

As a newcomer to the business I was still relying very heavily on advice from others at this time. I knew, usually, where I wanted to go, though not how to get there; and what I particularly wanted at this early stage was a new product or products that Sterling could manufacture while awaiting development from our own designer, Frank Waters. Much of the final decision-making was influenced by Major Frank Hobart, a lecturer on infantry weapons at the Royal College of Military Science, Shrivenham, and Rupert Pengelley of the *International Defense Review*, who was a friend from the HAC. Another particular source of help and advice was Colonel Ralph ('Bunny') Warren.

Formerly the British Defence Attaché in Berne, dapper and wearing a monocle, Bunny Warren was the UK representative for SIG (Schweizerische Industrie Gesellschaft). In February 1973 he took me over to Neuhausen am Rheinfall in northern Switzerland, where the company is based. Known for a diverse range of products including everything from small-arms to mining machinery and machine tools to railway carriages, the SIG factory is situated right on the Rhine Falls themselves – quite the most romantic setting. The small-arms then being produced at SIG were the elegant P210 pistol and the 7.5 mm Swiss Army Rifle. Large but comfortable to fire, the latter was an engineer's dream; it was solidly made with a complicated delayed blow-back mechanism. The factory was allowed to make only for the Swiss Government, as war material under the Swiss Constitution cannot be exported.

My interest was in the SIG designs and prototypes for a couple of new light-weight rifles which if produced outside Switzerland would obviously be capable of being exported. But I had come on the scene just too late. SIG had already signed an agreement with the French company Manurhin.

Bob Jennings and his colleagues, Hugh McWhinnie and David Wilson, also tried to interest me in several guns, including the M-10 and M-11 sub-machine gun designed by Gordon Ingram for Mitch Werbell's company, Military Armament Corporation of Powder Springs, Georgia. The Royal Marines' Special Boat Squadron had bought a small quantity, as they were the right weight to hang around the neck of a frogman. I was not impressed with the gun, which could not compare with the Sterling. However, it was compact and very inexpensive to produce, and perhaps my judgement was too harsh; I could have covered the whole spectrum of the sub-machine gun market. But in any event the licence fee was too high.

The same individuals brought me John Foote's FAC-70, a good simple 5.56 mm rifle, but it was only in the prototype stage and as such no use to me now. The special attraction of the Armalite rifle was that it was already tooled, and they were prepared to order a regular annual quantity for the US market.

Needless to say, I was in a very good position to see all kinds of new small-arms projects at this time, and one of the most impressive − although no offers to licence it were ever made − was the Thompson Ramo Woolridge Low Maintenance Rifle. This was an automatic open-bolt-firing rifle, on which the magazine protruded from one side − a huge advantage in military use, except possibly when it comes to arms drill.

Of the civilian projects offered to Sterling at the time, I particularly remember some good-looking twelve-bore shotguns, which incorporated a patent whereby the action was pulled open for loading and ejecting, and twisted for cocking, then closed for action. It was a remarkably simple mechanism but very effective. The approach was made by an Irishman named Kavanagh who had been an officer in the Parachute Brigade. However, Kavanagh seemed to be embroiled in some dispute with the police authorities in Cornwall where he lived. He had formerly produced guns in Ireland, running his own company, the Fenian Gun Company, until his son was murdered by terrorists. Politics apart, it was decided that as bird-shooting is such a traditional sport, a shotgun with such an unusual action would meet stiff consumer resistance. That our decision was right seems to be confirmed by the demise of the excellent French Darne shotgun.

I was also approached by the managing director of Cogswell & Harrison, the Piccadilly gunmakers. Coggies dabbled in the military market and in the past had given Sterling a few orders for sub-machine guns. They also represented the Czech arms agency, Omnipol, who posted a big bouncing Czech in their offices; it was an arrangement that suited all parties very well − particularly the Czech himself, who so thoroughly enjoyed the fleshpots and the good life available in London that he defected. Not surprisingly perhaps, Coggies then lost the agency. Their managing director was a man called Holden, Australian-born, who suggested to me that there was a good market for a British machine-made shotgun. BSA had ceased making their brute, and the Webley & Scott 700 was a shade too expensive for the trade. In short, the deal we were offered was a partnership whereby Coggies would provide their name and the engineering drawings, and Sterling would sink funds into financing the manufacture. The arrangement sounded good, until I realized that the drawings being supplied for a side-by-side shotgun were none other than those for the Brno. I might as well have done a deal direct with the Czechs.

While on the subject of shotguns, I had opened a dialogue with Don Mitchell, the President of High Standard in America, over the possibility of manufacturing their police slide-action shotguns. An annual figure of 40,000 was mentioned. Another of their designs that particularly interested me was the M-10 bull-pup automatic shotgun with plastic furniture; it was way ahead of its time. With David Howroyd I visited High Standard's plant in Hampden, Connecticut. We were impressed by their surface-broaching operations, which must have cost millions to tool up, but less impressed by the inordinately high scrap rate. We also worried that the company's financial future looked uncertain (and sure enough, the company disappeared from the market shortly afterwards).

Another visit to America took me to Sturm, Ruger & Company's plant at Southport, Connecticut. Bill Ruger was not too interested in any form of collaboration on guns, but he was keen that I should find him a partner in England to make the Ruger 'Speed Six', of which there were three prototypes in existence. This was not a gun, however, but a look-alike 1926 Bentley, except with modern running gear and a Ford V-8 six-litre engine. As far as I know, he never did find the partner he wanted.

Having considered the whole range of possibilities open to us, we finally agreed that the most attractive remained a collaboration with Armalite. Again David Howroyd and I flew to America, this time to Costa Mesa, California, to spend some time with George Sullivan, Chuck Dorchester and their colleague Dick Klotzly. We looked at Armalite's tooling for the AR-18 and David decided that it was capable of being refurbished at Sterling.

Our co-operation and licence agreement was eventually signed up in London in July 1974. Now the Sterling Armament Company of Dagenham, England, would be joining Armalite Inc. of California and Howa of Japan in manufacturing the AR-18 5.56 mm assault rifle. It was definitely a satisfying moment, signing that agreement with Armalite. But meanwhile, Sterling had run into a crisis.

CHAPTER SEVEN

Buyers, Sellers and South America

Throughout 1973, in fact ever since the deal Major Keen had secured with the Libyans, the order situation on the Marks 4 and 5 had been buoyant. Suddenly, in his infinite wisdom, Muammar Gaddafi opened his mouth and started sounding off about filthy British imperialists and the aid he was going to give to the IRA. Our licence to export the guns was abruptly revoked. Then, reasoning perhaps that Gaddafi's outburst had been intended more for home consumption, the authorities reinstated our licence. O frabjous day! But we had scarcely heaved a sigh of relief than Gaddafi opened his mouth again — and this time, as it happened, a German cargo ship called the *Claudia* was caught running arms off the Irish coast. That was that, as far as Sterling was concerned. There was no hope whatsoever of getting a licence now.

However, almost at the same time, late 1973, Iraqi troops started massing on the border with Kuwait. The Kuwaitis were desperate for Mark 4 Sterlings, and of course we were only too glad to supply them. A deal was arranged with the British Government, whereby we bought the last barrel casings from Donnington; we thus managed to make up a quantity of new guns which were immediately flown out to Kuwait. The Iraqis must have taken fright on that occasion, for they did not attack.

In the wake of the *Claudia*, the Libyans were extremely good to me. The Libyan Defence Attaché in London, Major Jabril Haddad — he looked very much like Clint Eastwood — pointed out that none of the arms on the gun-runners' ship were standard issue in the Libyan Armed Forces. (Subsequently, whenever Sterlings were used in terrorist shoot-outs, the Special Branch of London's

Metropolitan Police came to us with the serial numbers, from which we were able to check delivery details; no Libyan guns ever went astray). And the head of the Libyan purchasing mission in Paris, Colonel Mufta Dakhil – he was more like an Arab version of Rod Steiger – showed genuine concern lest the return of the deposit money should cause problems for the company; indeed he authorized that the money should stay in place for a whole year.

Thanks to the Libyans, first for their order, then for their financial compassion, I had just the time I needed to get Sterling really moving. So, whatever Libya's conduct on the international scene, I will always point out how much I appreciate their generous and open behaviour towards one struggling British company. Cynics may say there must have been some huge backhander. There was not. No agent was ever involved, so not even a pennyworth of commission was paid.

We invited Jabril Haddad to dinner at our home, but my wife rather tactlessly presented a menu of king prawns followed by medallions of pork – which poor Haddad, being a Muslim, had to forego; he was forced to smoke his way through dinner.

I was back to my original problem: how to raise new orders, and fast. There is no fixed pattern to the selling of defence equipment, except that the ingredients must include three things: an official order, a valid export licence and a confirmed (irrevocable) letter of credit. The licence was granted by the Department of Transport and Industry, on advice from the M.O.D. The letter of credit usually came through a City of London bank. But the orders might come from anywhere.

Some orders came direct from the customer country. Some were part of official tenders. Some arrived through the British M.O.D. or Crown Agents. Some came through accredited agents or buying officers. Some were simply fixed up by wheeler-dealers, with the incentive that commissions would be due all round. To a degree, there was always a question of whom to trust. When several approaches were made to us over a deal with a single country, we invariably wondered who was the good guy and who was the bad guy.

It often puzzled me that a country should bother to use agents at all. Certainly, some countries lack a civil service and organized procurement facilities; but I suspect that the main reason for using an agent is probably either sloth or corruption, or a mixture of the two. The inevitable upshot is that the country ends up paying more, because an agent naturally expects a fee. And there is another point. It is always much easier to sell on quality than on price. That is, the agent and his general tend to buy the best item on the market, regardless of cost. If there is any comeback, they can always say that the goods were expensive *because* they were the best; or alternatively, the goods might be unsatisfactory *but* they were the best the market could offer. Needless to say, on a higher price an agent can charge a higher commission.

I once appointed an agent to act for the company in a NATO country. He was a charming man, formerly an officer in the Royal Navy, and very well thought of by the M.O.D. Sales Division. But I'll never forget how our meetings were mostly devoted to structuring the possible commission payments and ensuring that they went through a Cayman Island company, which had been especially set up to hide the involvement of the head of the NATO country's navy.

If there is a secret to selling anything, it is never to be in a hurry. I knew that instinctively, and instinct was confirmed by experience. But it's not easy advice to follow, especially when the bank is threatening to appoint a receiver. And it does not mean one can delay the response to an initial enquiry. However tentative the buyer's first move, the seller should always respond immediately. British firms have a terrible reputation, in the international arms community at least, for doing nothing. Even a simple request for information can, if treated properly, turn into a long-term business relationship that is equally satisfying to both sides. Once the first response has been made, it is actually easier to play for time while sufficient information is gleaned to make a proper decision.

The relevant embassy or high commission can also be helpful, contrary to what some defence companies may claim. I invariably found the British defence or commercial attaché well informed and eager to assist. Naturally I would not expect them to supply me with intricate specialized information, perhaps about developments in the ballistics field; what I wanted from them was more general commercial information. They live and work in the country; they know the people, they hear the rumours, they check the facts. I made it a golden rule to contact them in advance and visit them whenever I arrived in a country, for an up-to-the-minute summary of whatever was going on in the area. Without exception, they were as co-operative as they were courteous.

And now, as I prepared to do a tour of South America, I found out just how helpful the British embassies can be.

When I bought the company, Sterling had only just started selling in South America: a fact for which we had one man to thank. His name was Andrés Neubauer and he lived in Chile, though he had fenced for Hungary in the 1936 Olympics. Elderly but energetic and very well connected, it was Andrés who had spurred the interest of the Chilean Armed Forces in the Mark 5 — which they then purchased.

But I never did visit Chile, or, for that matter, Paraguay or Uruguay. There was no point in my inviting orders if the British government then refused to grant us an export licence, for the Government's decision naturally was influenced by the possibility that sub-machine guns might be used in the suppression of human rights. Traditionally the most democratic of South American countries, Chile had been suffering economic chaos under the Marxist Dr Allende and then, in September 1973, had undergone the trauma of a military coup followed by the authoritarian rule of General Pinochet. Even if I had wanted to sell arms to Pinochet and his henchmen, I would never have been allowed to. The same applied to Paraguay under General Stroessner and also to Uruguay, racked by anarchist spasms and fierce repression.

As a result, it was to the British Embassies that I turned when collecting representation in South America, and they did not let me down.

Thus Sir Raymond Smith became our agent in Venezuela. Sir Raymond, who had been knighted for his services to British exports, lived in Caracas, the capital, where he was also the agent for Rolls-Royce and British Aerospace. Both he and his wife were avid art collectors, and furthered this passion through a large well-known gallery that they owned in Caracas. When in London, staying at Claridges where Sir Raymond would throw lavish parties for visiting Venezuelan service chiefs, they would spend any spare minute visiting galleries and exhibitions for new work. Shortly after meeting Sir Raymond, my wife and I happened to be at a dinner party when one of the guests, himself a gallery owner, recited how that week a woman had come in and announced herself as Lady Smith from Caracas. 'And I'm Robin Hood from Timbuktu,' he retorted. The next day he hot-footed it round to Claridges, armed with flowers and a profuse apology. The Smiths, fortunately, saw the funny side of it.

Later, in June 1974, when I was in Venezuela myself, I spent some time at Maracay, where the military factory Cavim (Compania Anónima Venezolana de Industrias Militares) made ammunition and assembled FAL rifles. Cavim were enthusiastic about assembling Sterlings too, but the project eventually had to be abandoned when the country's oil-based economy started to go wrong.

My wife was with me in Venezuela and we took the opportunity to travel around a bit. We visited the house in Caracas where the great South American hero, Simón Bolívar, had once lived (he was born in Caracas in 1783), and spent a day going over the mountains in a cable car to the town of La Guaira on the Caribbean coast.

Then Peru. Again thanks to the relevant British Embassy we had found an excellent agent: a lawyer named José Carlos Lofer d'Abreu. He was determined to outdo a friend of his who represented FN. In fact, before my visit to Peru we had had a visit at Dagenham from two Peruvian police generals. One of them, Oscar Olivares, claimed to have represented Peru at shooting at the Olympics, yet he was the only man, woman or child that I ever met who was quite incapable of handling a Sterling. He succeeded in shooting out the lights of the Sterling range, and might have done worse had not Major Keen relieved him of the weapon. Following the police generals' visit, Beavan Keen had gone to Peru to pave the way for me, and reckoned that there was a definite order for 10,000 Sterlings; he even helped to organize the finance. So when I reached Lima I went round to Olivares's office with high hopes. I was told to call back in an hour as the general was very busy. When I returned I saw the reason why; two tired-looking hookers were emerging from his office. After a respectable wait, I heralded my arrival and went in. Olivares was charm personified, but we never did receive the order. The contract was eventually won some years later by the Spanish firm of Star Echevarria, whose product was substantially cheaper than Sterling's.

Again we managed to enjoy our off-duty moments. José Carlos took us to a museum of pre-Columbian antiquities, set in a private park with a gun museum next door. The owner, one Senor Mujica, lived in a large mansion in another part of the park; apparently his drawing room was worth a visit, too, so we were taken in for a look. The room was vast, and filled with stuffed game animals and furniture made from animal parts. We were told, proudly, that all the animals had been shot by Senor Mujica. My wife is an ardent animal conservationist and winced when asked to sign the visitors' book. But tactfully she wrote, 'I just loved the floor' – which was indeed remarkable, made from round wooden blocks, sectioned tree trunks, and highly polished.

In Ecuador our agent was Mauricio Gandara, a diminutive lawyer and politician who had been through the military academy with many of the more influential army officers. He later became Ecuadorian Ambassador to the Court of St James in London. Mauricio had arranged the demonstration that I had to give in Quito. The range was just outside the city, beneath a cliff face. What worried me was that on top of the cliff there was a convent; my nerve nearly cracked when the assorted Ecuadorian army officers and other ranks started shooting the high-velocity Armalite rifles in full automatic fire.

Our next destination was Bolivia. I remember being impressed, when the aircraft touched down at La Paz airport, that the airport staff were standing by with oxygen bottles; at 14,000 feet it is the highest international airport in the world. But my first problem was not so much altitude sickness as lost vaccination certificates – I'd left them in Mauricio's car – without which I could not be allowed into the country. Luckily a solution was found. I was revaccinated, there and then; and I must say I'm very proud of the certificate, with its elaborate badge of Bolivia.

Mr de Roover, our agent in Bolivia, had arranged a demonstration for air force personnel the following day – which, in its way, was no less nerve-racking than the one in Quito. The range was marked out to the 200-yard mark: fine for the Armalite, but I had never before shot a Sterling at that distance. In fact there was only one hiccough. The ammunition I'd been given was 9 mm Parabellum all right, but it had been made in Germany in 1936. However, I used one box without trouble, then opened another and fed a thirty-four round magazine. Using a Mark 4, I settled down for some more shooting. My first two rounds missed. I had never missed before. I fired again, and missed again. Then again. On my fifth attempt there was a loud report and hot lead particles sprayed around the ejection port. Unloading the gun, I peered down the barrel: it was blocked. I took a cleaning rod and cleared five bullets from the barrel. then I continued with the demonstration, with much more satisfactory results. The 200-strong gathering of officers and men burst into applause. The Sterling really was a fine gun.

Our path in Bolivia was smoothed by a very pleasant American-educated Bolivian by the name of Frank Taendler who worked at the British Embassy. We did not, perhaps, see the country at its best, for we were there in winter and the weather was damp, cold and dull; but the greyness was relieved by the people in their bowler hats and multi-coloured ponchos.

On leaving Bolivia I was confident that we could expect a reasonable order from the military. Alas, by the time we arrived back in London there had been yet another change of government in Bolivia; as a result we were informed that export licences would not be forthcoming.

A much more successful part of the trip was in Argentina. We arrived at the airport for Buenos Aires to be met by the whole consortium of agents who would be representing us: Hugo Binstock, who had English antecedents and swore that his surname was a corruption of 'Winston'; William Arias, a well-manicured lawyer and politician; and two gunsmiths called Berlusconi and Murdoch. Berlusconi was still recovering from a guerrilla attack on his premises; fourteen 9 mm rounds had been removed from his body, though he looked remarkably fit to me. Charlie Murdoch was a third-generation Scot, huge and red-haired; I couldn't help laughing when he spoke not with a Scottish burr but an Argentinian accent. They had laid on the most impressive car to transport us to our hotel: an IKA-Renault Torino, powered by a four-litre Ford engine. It looked like a large Italian sports coupé, complete with wood panelling and leather seats.

Coincidentally, Berlusconi and Murdoch also represented High

Standard, the American shotgun manufacturer with the M-10 that I had liked so much. Both highly professional, they organized two excellent demonstrations where I was glad to be a mere spectator. After the demonstrations we were entertained to dinner by Captain Juan Carlos Herzberg, Commandant of the Argentinian Naval Commandos. The Navy was most definitely the senior service in Argentina, and the Commandos were an elite force, equivalent perhaps to the Royal Marine Commandos. We were delighted to find them most impressed by the Mark 5 silenced gun.

The next day we went out to an estancia some three hours' drive from Buenos Aires, past La Plata, and spent most of the time firing different weapons. In the evening we clambered aboard jeeps to shoot ground hogs or prairie dogs in the headlights.

I liked the country, and I liked the people, but Argentina was not a happy place just then. Even from our hotel room in Buenos Aires we could hear shooting in the streets at night. Government-backed gangs were let loose, apparently, to sort out the Montoneros (guerrillas). Isabelita Perón was still in power, ably assisted by her minister, López Rega, who was probably pulling the strings. However, Sterling did get some sizable orders from the Argentinians and, what's more, we also obtained export licences.

After Buenos Aires our trip was essentially over, though we had a week's holiday in Rio on our way home. My attention rarely wandered from the tanga bikinis on Copacabana beach. Brazil, unfortunately, never wanted any foreign-made small-arms, though I did have agents there later. Brazil was the preserve of Armalite, and the AR-18 had been thoroughly tested by the Brazilian Armed Forces. Armalite were quite convinced that they had a licence deal with the Brazilian Government firmly in the bag.

There is a postscript to this South American jaunt. When the Argentinians invaded the Falklands/Malvinas, colour photographs appeared in the British *Sunday Times* of Argentinian naval commandos all toting none other than the Mark 5 Sterling Patchett silenced gun L34A1. But I had to stifle my pride.

CHAPTER EIGHT

Expansion in Practice

With the Armalite agreement confirmed, in 1974, Frank Waters' designs for a Sterling 5.56 mm rifle were abandoned. He had actually produced two firing prototypes, which now lay dormant, though they were to be used again in time. Our priority now was to put the Armalite into production at Dagenham.

We would need more factory accommodation, however, so we started looking for suitable sites nearby; fortunately an extra 20,000 square feet of space was found on the very same factory estate. This was all arranged so speedily that I did wonder whether the space might lie idle and wasteful for too long; but I took the plunge and signed the lease. It just so happened that, even as the ink was drying on the lease, the Comet Discount Electrical Warehouse next door to us caught fire and was burnt down. How the flames did not engulf Sterling I will never know. But the upshot was that I leased over half the new premises to Comet, until they managed to rebuild their own, by which time the Armalites were in production and we could make full use of the space ourselves. I can refute any charges that it was a case of 'Jewish lightning', but I admit that the fire did happen at the most opportune moment!

The other requirement now was equipment. Standard machine tools were acquired at large auction sales and on them were mounted the special fixtures and tooling that produced the individual Armalite components. These fixtures, like elaborate vices, were designed with considerable ingenuity, to produce a highly accurate part without requiring exceptional skill from the operator. Particular thought went into the methods of drilling and machining the rifle's bolt and bolt carrier, the two most important components, and it was decided that both of these operations could be de-skilled and automated. In other words, the need to rely on skilled operators, irregular as any other human beings (not to mention more expensive than most), was removed and yet at the same time consistent quality could be guaranteed. To automate production fully, from raw material to finished component, would have cost millions of pounds; instead, it was decided to automate just those two stages.

The parts were presented as blanks to multi-station special-purpose machines, each station representing a separate skilled operation. The operator then pressed the button to start the automatic cycle and stood by to carry out the deburring operation by hand, smoothing off the rough and ragged edges caused by machining. At the end of the cycle he would manually move the parts from one station to the next and repeat the process; by the time he had finished with the component it was ready for blacking (metal finishing) and assembly. The end result was a component of remarkable precision and quality.

I found it most impressive, watching that high-precision machinery in action, automatically turning out a complicated piece of work. It moved quickly and surprisingly quietly, each different stage being preceded by a 'click'. The only concession to disorder was the white soluble cutting oil pouring wantonly all over it.

Armalite had passed on various instructions and suggestions, but we were curious when they specifically told us not to attempt certain changes in materials and also in methods of construction − changes that would have seemed to be logical improvements. Curiosity got the better of us, and we indulged in a few experiments; but Armalite had been absolutely right. The guns then became unreliable for reasons unaccountable in pure engineering terms.

To put the Armalite rifle into production took 15 months. Considering that we had to remake much of the existing tooling, and given our limited resources, it was a magnificent achievement.

Meanwhile, we had to fill all that extra factory space; we were very conscious of the need to spread our overheads. As a result, we brought in a number of other enterprises, such as Yaffle.

A small import-and-distribution firm, Yaffle was acquired from Charles Nickerson, son of the late Sir Joseph Nickerson, the wealthy Lincolnshire farmer and seed merchant whose interest in birds was matched only by his devotion to bird shooting. Yaffle (another name for the green woodpecker) represented Mauser in the United Kingdom and imported sporting rifles and shotguns and accessories. In profit terms it was a questionable venture, but it did teach us a lot about the gun trade. We recruited two or three gunsmiths, who produced some very fine English-style, hand-made, over-and-under shotguns. I had these on display at one of the game fairs, the annual showcase for the field sporting kind, and they attracted no little attention. In fact, the guns were compared directly with those of Boss & Co; obviously Boss had the name, but their guns were five times the price. However, since queues were not forming to place deposits on them, I called a halt to the operation, completed ten, and sold them all to Bruce Hunt III of Atlanta Outfitters Inc. It is to my eternal regret that I did not keep one of them; they were superb.

Yaffle continued by selling Benelli shotguns and also German air rifles, imported from large German distributors, and undercut the accredited agents in Britain. Eventually, this new activity spurred Sterling into producing its own airgun, which proved to be highly successful.

In addition, by this time — some four or five years since I had taken over — we had been awarded the M.O.D. spares order. However, this was not the cause for rapture that it might seem, firstly because the order was much smaller than we would have hoped, and secondly because it was made in such a grudging spirit. Understandably perhaps, the M.O.D.'s holding of Sterling Sterlings was being cannibalized, the parts being used for spares wherever possible. Much more regrettable was the fact that the M.O.D. saw fit to have us 'cost investigated'. Ministry officials were quartered on the company to examine every single component and analyse its material content and production time. Our records were impeccable and, in spite of trying every trick in the book, the men from the Ministry found no possible reductions. The contract was awarded, worth around £100,000; but this mean little operation, prompted no doubt by some penny-wise cost-cutting whim, must have cost the M.O.D. as much again.

It was not enough, though. Even with the spares contract, and even when the Armalite was well into production, we had to keep up the quest for new work as a back-up. I decided to approach the Royal Small-Arms Factory (RSAF) at Enfield.

I had been told, but refused to believe, that there was still a lingering resentment about the success Sterling and Patchett had scored over the M.O.D. in the case of the Mark 4 patents. After all, it had been concluded ten years before, and the M.O.D. were demonstrably in the wrong. I was confident that any feelings of ill will would have faded. Besides, the M.O.D. would surely see the sense in using a tried and trusted company like Sterling for sub-contract work. And anyway, if either party had cause to nurse a grievance it was Sterling, and not merely because of the Patchett patents. The particular thorn in our flesh was the relationship between the British Government and the German arms manufacturer, Heckler & Koch of Oberndorf near Stuttgart.

Founded in 1948, originally to produce sewing machines, Heckler & Koch then switched to armaments and by the late 1950s they were making the G-3 rifle. When West Germany was allowed to re-arm, the Bundeswehr first adopted the Belgian FAL (Fusil automatique légère) rifle; however, German designers had worked on the delayed blowback action – the system developed by CETME (Centro de Estudios Técnicos de Materiales Especiales) in Spain and favoured by Heckler & Koch – and the West Germans decided in 1959 that they preferred the G-3. The gun was cheaper to produce than the FN FAL and became very successful. Heckler & Koch sold it extensively, setting up licensed manufacturing to various degrees in about ten countries, usually in partnership with the government of the host country. However, post-war Germany was forbidden to supply arms to those countries contiguous with the state of Israel, and when the kingdom of Jordan wanted to buy 25,000 G-3s the Jordanian authorities approached Sterling's Major Keen, Sterling having already supplied them with sub-machine guns. After much dialogue between Dagenham and Oberndorf, an agreement was reached: the rifles should be assembled in Dagenham and marked up as Sterling G-3s. Then the British Foreign Office threw a spanner in the works. The deal was off. For some incomprehensible reason, they baulked at the idea of Sterling supplying German-designed rifles to Jordan. Of course Jordan got her G-3s by some other route. All that happened was that Sterling and U.K. Ltd had been deprived of the profit from that deal.

And then the British Government set up an association between Heckler & Koch and the RSAF Enfield.

In the early 1970s, Heckler & Koch were trying to promote their MP-5 sub-machine gun, which used some common parts with the G-3 rifle and worked on the same delayed blowback principle. They marketed it as a 'modern' sub-machine gun although its development was as old as the Sterling's. They made great play of the fact that it did not have a side-loading magazine − despite the known advantages of such a magazine. A side magazine rests on the forearm and is almost like another grip, offering the firer more stability and hence more accuracy. Furthermore, the firer can lie absolutely flat when using a weapon with a side-mounted magazine. But the MP-5's real problem lay in the delayed blowback system itself, which, on account of its complicated bolt arrangement, makes the weapon very sensitive to the ingress of sand, mud and other dirt. Only in parade ground conditions can the MP-5 be relied upon to function consistently.

However, Heckler & Koch had two outstanding skills. The first was fine engineering; they made presentable small-arms out of a lousy original design. The second was their mastery of the art of good marketing. Somehow they persuaded the British Government that the RSAF Enfield ought to assemble their sub-machine gun.

It was ludicrously unfair to Sterling. By imposing a 'Preferred Source Policy', the MOD simply barred any competition with the RSAF Enfield; whenever the British Government decided to invite tenders in the small-arms field, Sterling were allowed to bid only if the RSAF did not wish to do so. But, unfair though it was, we had learned to live with that. What I could not accept was that Enfield, from behind the protection of British Government policy, were now entering a commercial alliance with a foreign company − and, moreover, a company that they knew to be in direct competition with a British company. In plain English, they were actively undermining Sterling's position.

Naturally I expressed my concerns to the M.O.D. The 'Preferred Source Policy', as operated, was manifestly unfair. In response I was given every assurance that Enfield were acting only as commercial subcontractors to Heckler & Koch, and that they most certainly would not be handling sub-machine guns in any shape or form.

Within a year I had personally seen Heckler & Koch MP-5 sub-machine guns in two of the Gulf States: only a few, but all with the tell-tale Enfield marking on the side, 'EN'. Their origin, although hotly denied by the M.O.D., was confirmed to me privately by three different people who had left their employment at Enfield. Furthermore, in the course of my travels I was informed by defence attachés in the British Embassies or High Commissions in no fewer than ten different countries that a confidential circular had been sent exhorting overseas staff to promote the sale of Heckler & Koch small-arms. And there was a postscript at the bottom of the page, in small letters, to the effect that Sterling still made a sub-machine gun. The defence attachés were, to a man, even more annoyed than I!

Almost as ludicrous is the SAS connection, though one criticizes that *élite* body at one's peril. In the field of small-arms, the SAS rejects whatever is standard in the British Army or available from British sources. Certainly, it would appear that SAS soldiers are the only ones who cannot jump through a window with a loaded Sterling. The side-loading magazine, apparently, gets in the way. There are no prizes for guessing what their preference is: the Heckler & Koch equivalent. The SAS and their West German counterparts, GSG-9, have formed a mutual admiration society which encourages uniformity of equipment – and German weaponry is favoured every time. Yet after the SAS had stormed the Iranian Embassy in London, there were reports that one of the Heckler & Koch MP-5s did indeed jam.

One day when I was a guest at the Special Forces Club in Knightsbridge, I was introduced to a lieutenant-colonel who was in command of one of the SAS wings. When he heard that I was managing director of Sterling he exclaimed that he was in the same line of business. Puzzled, I asked what he meant.

'Well, we sell Heckler & Koch guns,' he said. 'We've already sold five million marks' worth this year.'

I was stunned. How could a serving British officer be involved commercially? And how could he be so naïve? I suspect that he did not realize he was compromising his position. It is just possible that the Government had given him the go-ahead. If so, with the SAS as their free demonstration team, it's little wonder that Heckler & Koch managed to sell even their inferior product.

Despite the RSAF Enfield's attitude, their director accepted an invitation to visit Sterling. In one way or another I was determined to break down the old ill-feeling and to win Sterling some sub-contract work. In 1979 the director of Enfield arrived. He showed great interest in everything he saw, but no sub-contract work was ever forthcoming.

However, some three or four years later, Enfield produced prototypes for a lightweight rifle: a bull-pup design (the trigger group is positioned in front of the breech area by a linkage, so that the rifle needs only a minimal butt and is hence much shorter in length). On display at the British Army Equipment Exhibition, the prototype's operation looked suspiciously like that of the AR-18. In fact, when our designer, Frank Waters, was allowed to disassemble it, his first remark was, 'Well, here's an old friend.' Sure enough, the 'new' rifle utilized our bolt and bolt carrier, and our magazine.

It took Enfield nearly a decade to get that rifle into production, the SA 80/85 as it became known: years and years of work, plus approximately one hundred million pounds of public money. They had appalling teething troubles with it and, judging by some of the remedies they tried out (such as three guide rods for the bolt carrier), they obviously fell headlong into some of the traps that Armalite had warned us against. And, to add petty insult to injury, we discovered that Hodgson & Sanders, builders of special-purpose machine tools, had been called in to supply Enfield with the self-same machines that had been developed between Sterling and themselves.

The SA 80/85's bull-pup design (lacking a stock) gave only a questionable advantage, as Enfield ought to have known: they had produced the EM-2, also a bull-pup though of sturdier construction, which had suffered a breech explosion during testing, the firer losing half his face. One of the directors of the Belgian firm, Fabrique Nationale, told me that they would never make bull-pup weapons. However good the quality of the gun's manufacture, faulty ammunition could result in a complete loss of confidence in it. Furthermore, nearly 20% of all shooters are left-handed, but the SA 80/85 cannot be fired left-handed because of the ejection port. Add to that the fact that the 5.56 mm/.223″ round is an extremely high-velocity/high-powered round, and the idiocy becomes clear:

the SA 80/85 is a very poor gun, based on 30-year-old technology. It is also very expensive. It cost well over the $500 mark. By way of contrast, in 1982 a Lebanese friend took me over to Colt, who undertook to sell us the M-16A1 at a price that would have worked out at just $120 a piece. For a quarter of the price, the British could have had a better rifle, plus commonality of parts with their most powerful ally. To any normal mortal being, that would have made a certain amount of sense.

But, during my time at Sterling, sense seemed to be just one of the qualities lacking in the British Government's attitude towards small-arms. As odd as it seems, the Government behaved as though it wanted to kill off all armament production in private hands; certainly, the circular encouraging defence attachés to promote Heckler & Koch weapons seems to indicate a distinct wish to be rid of Sterling. Could it be because the private operations were so much more efficient? At that time the Government operation did not even have to pay its way. Things have changed today; most military production has been privatized, though vacillation and defence cuts have resulted in most companies having to rethink their *modus operandi*, and there are complaints that the general standard of equipment entering service with the British armed forces has fallen.

I am not in favour of privatization of the Royal Ordnance Factories. They were never really 'nationalized', and never had commercial restraints but were part of the M.O.D. Since the Ministry, almost exclusively, funded their production and their research and development, they should have remained part of the M.O.D. If a country is to remain a major military power, it must produce its own military equipment and armour, like the USA and France. But perhaps in the military context, by opting out of this responsibility, the British Government intended privatization to be a step on the road towards a United States of Europe. That may well be the right way forward, but it was gutless not to say so out loud. The British taxpayer ought to know where his money is going − and there can't be many who are happy to subsidize a foreign company to the commercial detriment of home-grown industry.

Despite the ill-will we met in some official quarters, I should add that other authorities continued to co-operate with Sterling. The police, for instance, continued to provide escorts for deliveries of any quantity of arms to the docks or airports, or to and from the Proof House where the barrel of every weapon has to be tested by law. For our part, we supplied expert evidence to the police when they were prosecuting a registered firearms dealer, in a test case involving the possession of a 'police carbine'. This was the special version of the Mark 4 Sterling that was designed for use only as a semi-automatic: an attempt to obviate disaster in the hands of inexperienced or panicky personnel in overseas police forces. Unfortunately the police managed to foul up the case; but that was their problem, not ours.

At the time, semi-automatic weapons were still permitted to those with the appropriate licence. A determined gun fancier could easily obtain such weapons from one source or another, though Sterling felt that it was in everybody's interest not to sell these weapons in Britain. As a company, Sterling did not want the aggravation of small quantity orders. Furthermore, by the adept use of a file, the carbine could be converted to fully automatic fire. Indeed, Sterling had a convention with the police that the carbines would not be offered for sale on the home market, and the police appreciated the gesture. However, I do know of at least one registered dealer who obtained an export licence and ordered a carbine from Sterling – then kept it, in spite of assurances to the contrary. There was nothing we could do. The law was only tightened up some years later, following the tragedy at Hungerford.

CHAPTER NINE

God Bless America!

For gun manufacturers, the world military market is a big pool but fraught with peril. Every country strives wholeheartedly to support and encourage its own indigenous armaments industry. That generally includes at least a degree of financial help, sometimes to the extent that there is over-production resulting in the inevitable price-cutting. Most countries actively promote their own arms on the world market. Furthermore, some countries use arms as an instrument of foreign policy: arms are given away free of charge in order to secure some specific political end. For a commercial company like Sterling, entering the world market against such political competitors could be like swimming against the tide in shark-infested waters. However, there is a very large gun market where those political risks are minimal, and that is the American civilian market.

This market always interested me, although it took a long time before I began to understand it. As a foreigner, even though I spoke nearly the same language as the natives, I found some aspects of the American way very puzzling. Also, much of what was available on the US civilian market was sought after by some military markets – semi-automatic weapons, sights and night-vision equipment, for instance. Anyone shopping for arms in America could find the source of what they wanted in *Shotgun News*, a trade publication which in fact contained only a few pages on shotguns. Many of the arms in Northern Ireland, in both U.D.F. and I.R.A. hands, have been acquired through this channel.

It is true that some of the American gun companies are very large and powerful, but the fact remains that the American market is open to all comers. Irrespective of who is the producer, a good unique gun will always do well.

From the start of my time at Sterling I was eager to find opportunities in America that we could exploit. There had been odd sales already and the Marks 4 and 5 had dribbled on to the police market, but I wanted more. Armalite looked at the problem for us, and pointed out that federal law expressly stated that guns with an automatic capability could be sold only to the law enforcement agencies. In other words, we could only hope to sell specially constructed Sterlings in the semi-automatic mode in the general distribution field. But here we faced another problem: our guns, so reliable and so well made, were too expensive for the general market. On the other hand, we found that the Sterling was held in very high regard in America, and some interesting approaches were made.

One approach was from Robert Imel of PAWS (Police Automatic Weapons Systems) who was keen to manufacture the Mark 4 under licence in Oregon. Initially we were doubtful; he appeared to be merely a private citizen without too much in the way of funds. The tooling at Sterling had cost hundreds of thousands of pounds, many years before. It seemed highly unlikely that Imel would be able to meet the huge initial cost. David Howroyd and I felt that morally we could not take any money, but, if Imel was hell-bent on producing a Sterling, it would be good publicity. We therefore invited him to come and spend a week working at Sterling. He would either see the enormity of the task, and be deterred, or he would learn something which should be of significant help to him. He duly came, and though he was apparently undeterred we heard nothing further for some time; then years later he started producing a simplified version of the Mark 4.

Another approach was from a young man, fresh-faced and tubby, who was a partner in Parker Arms of Texas. His name was Roma Skinner and he wanted to represent the company in the USA. He also put forward an idea to supply the Sterling with a 16-inch barrel − twice the length of our standard barrel − which would use a separate firing pin and fire from the closed-bolt position. Thence it would be virtually impossible to convert the gun back again to fully automatic fire. The idea clearly had potential. We agreed that proper plans should be drawn up and developed, with a view to Parker Arms then exploiting the American market.

Roma and his partner, a Chinese American called Kenny Yee, had adapted the idea from the Uzi, a new version of which was now selling in America and which effectively dodged the restrictions on normal sub-machine guns. I therefore contacted Mitch Kalter, of Action Arms Inc., who had done a very good job importing the Israeli Uzi. My idea was that Kalter should market the Sterling alongside the Uzi. I suggested that, although the Sterling and the Uzi were dire rivals, the chances were that many Americans would buy both if available. Besides, there must have been plenty of anti-Semitic Americans who would want a Sterling in preference. Mitch Kalter took it all in good spirit, and agreed with my marketing principle; but he could not risk upsetting Israeli Military Industries with whom he had some kind of exclusive arrangement.

Roma Skinner's idea turned into the Mark 6 Sterling, a semi-automatic with a long barrel. In 1982 we exhibited it at a shot show in Dallas, Texas, and it provoked immediate interest. At that time we still had to obtain final approval for the gun from the Bureau of Alcohol, Tobacco and Firearms; but the Bureau officials were extremely helpful and eventually the gun was passed.

Unfortunately, there were serious differences between the Parker Arms partners. Kenny Yee was the commercial strength, but Roma Skinner had the expertise in firearms and also the knowledge of the market. I warned Kenny that if he forced me to make a choice, I would have to go with Roma. After a very strained meeting (at which, according to Roma, Kenny had his hands on a loaded pistol), I parted from Kenny and, with Roma, set up a new company to trade solely in the products of the Sterling Armament Company.

Alas, Sterling could never use its own name in America because there was already a company called Sterling Arms Inc., a pistol producer in up-state New York. I met their president, Gene Sauls, at a shot show. An amiable man, he admitted that when they had started the company they looked at the names of many European companies, checked out which ones were not registered in America, and then simply picked the one they liked the best: Sterling.

Thus was born Lanchester USA Inc.

The reason why we established the separate American company was that I wanted to sell direct to the dealers.

At one time, in the early 1970s, the American firearms business was based on a three-step distribution system. The factory or importer sold guns to the distributor; the distributor sold to the dealer; the dealer retailed to the customer. The whole structure was based on the allocation of fine handguns (namely Smith & Wesson and Colt); these were the ones that were most in demand, and in order to obtain these a dealer would have to give *all* his business – including rifles and ammunition – to a single distributor. On occasions, the dealer was forced to take other merchandise as well, if he wanted to maintain or improve his position on the distributor's allocation list. Not surprisingly, the dealers were unhappy about this arrangement. Then the Gun Control Act of 1968 stopped direct mail of guns to the private individual, which reinforced the regional distributor system by making the dealer the only source of arms and ammunition for non-licensed individuals. In 1968 there were approximately 90,000 federal gun dealers. By 1981 this figure had doubled. However, the new licensed dealers were not gunstores but private individuals, who had obtained the licence in order to make private purchases at wholesale prices. Also, several new distributors entered the business just to cater for these part-time dealers. The new distributors sold used guns, surplus ammunition and some new guns from the smaller manufacturers, but they could not supply Colts or Smith & Wessons as these were allocated to the regional distributors.

In 1980/81 the whole situation blew up. The economic recession caused a slow-down in demand, allowing handgun companies to catch up with orders. But Smith & Wesson kept up their production rate. The regional distributors kept ordering at the same rate, and tried to force the dealers to take up the slack. When the dealers reduced their orders to match the slow sales, the regional distributors tried to break purchase contracts that they had made with Smith & Wesson the previous year; but most of them were forced to take at least a portion of their allotment. Smith & Wesson, faced with a mounting inventory, then went to the national distributors and sold to them for the first time, in an effort to keep the supply line going. Now all the 100,000-plus dealers, who were licensed for their hobby, could buy Smith & Wessons at wholesale prices. This obviously hurt the bona fide gunstores, which no longer had an exclusive preserve. And the regional distributors could not reduce their inventories because of the price wars the national distributors were waging. The result was a series of bankruptcies and a widespread depression throughout the whole of the American firearms industry.

Slowly the lessons began to be learnt. Several manufacturers started to sell dealer-direct, in order to control the price of their product (by cutting out one step in the distribution process) and so be more competitive.

For foreign manufacturers the position was even more difficult. Alongside the more competitively priced American guns, imported guns now seemed impossibly expensive, the prices inflated by overseas shipping, customs duties and importer mark-ups. Many potential customers were put off European arms simply by the price.

It was the combination of factors, the three-tier distribution system and the prohibitive retail price, that persuaded me it would be sensible to own at least the first stages in the chain, the importing and initial distribution stages. That is why Lanchester was formed; to be able to reach the dealers direct.

There was another American connection; the partnership between Sterling and Asferonics Inc. of Leesburg, Virginia, the company that made Scotos sights. The Scotos was really the first of the military night sights, strong and sturdy enough to withstand the inevitable knocks of active service. Although other night-vision equipment existed at the time (the mid '70s), it was generally delicate and fragile, intended more for camera accessories. The image-intensifier tubes, which magnified any available light by 50,000 times, were bought in from RCA, the film, camera and record company; the rest of the equipment was manufactured and assembled in Leesburg, in a small but ultra-clean factory.

That area of Virginia and the Shenandoah Valley is my favourite part of America. When I first went there it all seemed strangely familiar, probably because I studied the American Civil War in some detail at school. I have a forebear by the name of James Brown Edmiston, a Scot who went to live in Charleston, South Carolina, where he owned a shipyard building wooden craft.

Needless to say, at the first signs of war my ancestor legged it back to Scotland. But the thought that I might have been a Southerner always biased my judgement of the Civil War. My ancestor, however, did leave his name indelibly printed on the memory of the Scottish public. He built some houses in Glasgow, long since demolished, but his name remained on the street signs. Glasgow Rangers play football in Edmiston Drive.

I twice visited Leesburg to meet the president of Asferonics, an optical engineer called Q Johnston, large, good-natured and righter-than-right-wing. Although he was no relation, he was funded by the Johnson & Johnson (baby oil and powder) empire. On my second visit my wife was with me, and we spent a delightful day on the Johnson & Johnson stud farm, Shenstone Farm, as guests of vice-president Richard Stokes and his wife. I was looking forward to a long and successful collaboration with Asferonics, but, not long after our visit, Q was killed by a truck. With his demise the company ceased to exist.

The Scotos was the first of many night-vision systems that were spawned in the USA and Western Europe. Superiority in night vision and thermal imaging gave an enormous advantage over Eastern Bloc countries — as underlined by the speedy victory in the 1991 Gulf war over the Soviet-supplied forces of Saddam Hussein. However, it is a fair bet that everyone has learnt that same lesson now; the question is whether the West can maintain that superiority.

CHAPTER TEN

Pipe Dreams

The principle of 'nothing ventured, nothing gained' is probably my greatest boost to motivation. That, and a reluctance to sit around doing nothing while waiting for things to happen. Things have to be made to happen. Not only does this keep frustration at bay, it usually also brings some sort of bonus in the form of useful information.

In other words, I was always looking for ways to expand the company, improve our profits and reduce overheads. Once we had started to expand production in Britain, my thoughts turned to acquisitions overseas.

One of Sterling's products was a conversion kit for the Number 4 Enfield rifle, to change it from .303" to 7.62 mm calibre. Of those parts of the kit that had to be bought in, the major part was the barrel, which was too long for us to manufacture on our own machines; instead it was purchased from Canons Delcour SA in Belgium. Georges Delcour had a splendid factory full of specialist machinery, such as rotary swaging and barrel-hammering machines, set in the heart of the Belgian countryside. On a visit I was shown around the factory and then entertained to lunch – always a pleasure in Belgium – along with two directors from the Italian firm of Luigi Franchi SpA. Although Luigi Franchi possessed advanced barrel-manufacturing capacity of their own, they still relied for some products on Delcour, whose diverse range of customers included the mighty FN and Holland & Holland. The upshot of that encounter was that the two directors, Marcello Puppi and Tullio Maroni, invited David Howroyd and me to visit their factory at Brescia, in northern Italy.

It occurred to me that we might be able to assemble Sterlings in Italy, to sell the Mark 5 silenced gun to the Italian Government under the noses of Beretta (whose Model 12 sub-machine gun could not be effectively silenced on account of its telescoping bolt construction).

Luigi Franchi themselves used to make a sub-machine gun, the LF-57, which was sold to the Italian navy. They also made major sub-assemblies for the MG-42 (Rheinmetall) machine gun, which had been sub-licensed and adopted by the Italian armed forces. But their best known products were shotguns, which from a mechanical point of view were extremely well made. They had an automatic chrome-plating facility for the barrel and a very clever patent for automatic engraving of shotgun bodies. It was some kind of electro-chemical etching/photographic process, but it allowed deep engraving on steel; also, it was not restricted to a flat surface but could follow the curves and angles of a shotgun receiver. The company also had a sintering (powdered metallurgy) plant for very high production runs of sub-contract work for the automotive industry.

Our visit, though interesting, proved fruitless. To the embarrassment of our hosts, some of the labour force were working to rule and most of the plant had been closed down. We gathered that there had been protracted trouble of this sort, and, probably as a result, the company ran into difficulties, was sold, and the management changed. I had wanted to buy their side-by-side actions (for double-barrel shotguns with barrels that lie side by side), which we could finish and stock in England, but as it turned out they made only automatics and over-and-unders (with one barrel set above the other). In any case, the Italian Government proved less than welcoming towards the Sterling Mark 5, and it would probably have sold only in limited quantities. Thus the Italian idea came to naught.

However, another idea took me to Canada. A South African friend had put Eddie Gagnée, a Canadian, in touch with me over the possible purchase of Valcartier (pronounced locally as Val cat see) Industries, outside Quebec. Gagnée and I flew over to view the plant. They were making ammunition by rather antiquated methods, but had some other interesting products like snow-mobiles. However, I found myself in the middle of a battle between provincial and federal governments, and backed out quickly. On the face of it, we might have had a remarkably good deal there – but not as a political football.

Another potential acquisition that was offered to me was Manufrance, the largest civilian gun company in France. Based in the singularly unexciting town of St Etienne, near Grenoble, but sited in an old and historic five-storey factory, the company was manufacturing shotguns (over-and-under, side-by-side and automatic), .22″ rifles, and bicycles. It also had a mail-order catalogue operation. After examining the company's position in some detail, I decided 'that if we could acquire the gun side, we would be able to assemble some Sterlings and Armalites in France and thus get a toehold in Francophone Africa. Banque Stern, the French bank, were prepared to support this plan and the French themselves were enthusiastic, as it meant that some 'anglicized' versions of their side-by-side shotguns might be sold in Britain. The only question was whether the plan would win French Government approval.

With so much hingeing on this single factor, I was hauled off to the Ministry of the Interior in the Rue Faubourg Saint Honoré, Paris. The Minister's office was appointed with Louix XV furniture; it was sumptious, more like a Colefax & Fowler showroom. Although I can, with practice, speak passable French, I let the Minister talk to me in English. The great problem, he explained, was that my plan was against the law. The ownership of war material was not allowed in private hands, and sub-machine guns were war material. Thinking of a parallel, albeit larger situation, I asked about Monsieur Dassault and his Mirage aeroplanes.

'That is different, monsieur. He's French.'

I had to see the funny side of it, but that, effectively, was where the conversation ended. I think the Minister saw the funny side too, but he could not admit to it. One cannot help but like the French in spite of the fact that they often seem such jerks, possibly because they retain that ingrained peasant outlook on life.

Yet another foreign bargain that I missed was brought to me by an American, Elliot Kulick. A lawyer who had been at Brasenose College, though well before my time, he had been asked by banking contacts to look into the possibility of investing in an American company whose only asset was a Belgian arms manufacturer, Mécar SA. In spite of being overladen with debt, Mécar had some good assets. They made Energa rifle grenades, a 90 mm gun and ammunition, and bazooka ammunition. The product line was ageing, and the main competition was from other Belgian companies, but the Belgian embassies abroad had been extremely helpful in securing new orders. Mécar was headed up by the chairman of the American company that owned it, Marvin Ruffin, who later took over the day-to-day running of the company himself. Again, I backed out, deterred by the relatively high Belgian wages and also by the strength of the Belgian unions (which had some very justifiable powers to prevent asset stripping). In the event, Mécar outlasted a couple of its rivals and Ruffin turned it around and made a spectacular financial success of the operation.

These near-misses occurred over a period of several years, and by no means dented my appetite for foreign expansion. But at the same time, I was casting around for other opportunities.

Being a manufacturer of something consumable had its appeal. The trouble with the Sterling was that it was built to last forever. The trigger mechanism, which was instantly removable anyway, was still made entirely of stainless steel. The same belt-and-braces philosophy was evident throughout the gun's entire construction. That was, of course, one of its assets. However, considering how many of the guns were in service, the spares requirements were minimal; with profits in mind, we sometimes wished it was otherwise. So when the prospect arose of our taking over a fireworks factory, I was particularly keen; here was a real consumable.

In fact, the fireworks included military pyrotechnics – flares, smoke and stun grenades and the like – and the company involved was Brocks Fireworks. They had a good name in the industry, and they had started to collect some good people who were orientated towards military requirements. The company had premises in Swaffham, Norfolk, and in Sanquhar, Dumfries. The shares were dispersed amongst the Brock family. There was no overall shareholders' aim or ultimate direction, but the working directors were eager that I should acquire a controlling interest; then at least they would know where they were going, and the selling and marketing overhead of two companies in the same field, Sterling and Brocks, would be combined.

The controller of one block of family shares was supportive, but a young member of the family saw this as his opportunity to shake the whole thing up and do it himself. I refused to go into a Dutch auction on the shares, especially when I might get caught in a family feud. Once again, I decided that the better part of valour was discretion.

In fact, Athol Mowbray, the sales executive, and the working directors, Arthur Read and Chris Gumbley, resolved to do their own thing, and we all agreed to stay in touch. Not long afterwards they made contact and asked me to join them in their acquisition of Astra Fireworks. Unfortunately, at the time they asked me I was having difficulties of my own, as will become clear, and for me Astra became another of the fish that got away.

Almost concurrently with the Brocks situation, Don Mitchell, who had been marketing our Sterling Armalite AR-180 rifles in America, presented me with another opportunity. At a shot show in Atlanta, Georgia, he introduced me to Wayne Baker of Freedom Arms Inc., which had made some interesting gun products in the past and now was concentrating on the manufacture of .22" LR mini revolvers in stainless steel. After building new premises and sorting out some teething problems in production, Freedom Arms had run into a cash crisis. They were thinking about selling out a majority, but needed an assurance on further investment to develop new products, such as the fearsome Casull .454" Magnum single-action revolver.

My interest was quickly kindled and four months later, in April, 1982, I took the Sterling company secretary, Keith Cole, to investigate further.

Freedom Arms was based in the small town of Freedom, on the Wyoming/Idaho border. Star Valley, which included Freedom, was like Switzerland; even in April there was still snow on the ground and we had great fun trying out skidoos. The local population, some 1,500 strong, boasted not only the Freedom Arms gun factory, but also a Swiss cheese factory and the famous Pitts aircraft factory. I was show round the Pitts factory, where they were building aerobatic biplanes of wood, canvas and dope; I suppose the work-force got used to it, but sniffing the dope gave me a high throughout my visit. The planes were of superb quality, justly renowned throughout the world.

There were no hotels in Freedom, and so we had been invited to stay with Wayne and Mariam Baker. Like nearly everyone in that area, they were members of the Church of Jesus Christ of Latter-day Saints, better known as Mormons. I knew nothing about Mormons then, except what I had read in a novel by Sir Arthur Conan Doyle, and expected something between the Ku Klux Klan, the Masons and the Amish; and I don't know much more now, except that the Bakers did not serve alcohol or coffee. What the house did contain was provisions and arms and ammunition enough to sit out the Third World War and its aftermath.

On the business side, Freedom Arms did not seem to need us. It would have been difficult to run from afar, and besides, we already had Armalite selling the AR-180 rifles and Lanchester starting on the Sterlings. Wayne Baker had more or less cracked his own problem and it would not take much more to get the whole enterprise humming. Sterling could not really contribute anything of substantial benefit, and we could not expect anything much in return; Freedom's products were designed to appeal chiefly to the American civilian market. We parted as friends, however, and have remained friends, and Freedom Arms has flourished on its own ingenuity and resources.

Returning from that trip, I was carrying a high-velocity rifle that had been designed by Dick Casull, chief designer for Freedom Arms, which I wanted to have evaluated at Sterling. Naturally I had to declare the article to Customs at Heathrow airport, and expected the usual long wait while bureaucratic formalities were unravelled. In fact, the delay was enlivened by some impromptu entertainment from a well-known diminutive comedian who happened to be in front of me in the queue. He had apparently acquired a new set of golf clubs, possibly as a gift, but he had been plucked from the 'Green' exit and was now being hammered for the full value of the clubs. The grim-looking Customs officer was treated to some of the funniest ad-libbing I have ever heard, but he closed his ears. The unfortunate comedian had to pay up.

If there is a moral about all those possibilities and their failure to materialize, it is that they did not go ahead for quite mundane reasons. For me they turned out to be pipe dreams, but only because of the most trivial circumstances. They might quite easily have gone ahead. All the plants were capable of military production, and were available to anyone with the funds − and comparatively meagre funds would have sufficed. Any outsider could have walked in off the street and bought himself a military production company.

At the time, only the French were apparently alert to the problem. In Britain and North America, anyone at all could have bought a gun company and started producing weapons for himself and his friends; and who was to know if those friends had terrorism in mind?

CHAPTER ELEVEN

New Products

A. J. R. (Sandy) Cormack had written to the company. He was already known as a writer on various aspects of small-arms (mainly military) and their design, and I was interested to meet him. We discovered that his family had lived in the same Edinburgh street as my grandparents, a complete coincidence. Although he himself was not a designer, he had some good ideas for new designs, and he also had a good knowledge of the military market and general trends in firearms. He had another trait that could be both valuable and uncomfortable at the same time: he was never afraid to speak his mind. Some of his ideas tallied with our own, and the upshot was that Sandy joined Sterling as an advisor.

In conjunction with Frank Waters, Sandy made a significant contribution to the further development of our range of products. As well as the Mark 6 Carbine, with its 16-inch barrel and close-bolt firing operation, designed to satisfy the requirements of American law, we now had a Mark 7, also known as the Para Pistol. This was a version of the Sterling without a stock and with part of the barrel casing cut away to give it the appearance of a pistol. Again, it was inspired by the Israeli-produced Uzi pistol.

We were also continuing to produce Armalites, of course. Apart from the AR-18 automatic rifle, Armalite had come up with a self-loading single-shot version, the AR-180, and also a machine carbine version called the AR-18S. The latter was a good-looking weapon with a gangster-like foregrip, but the combination of the high-velocity round and a shcrt 12-inch barrel made it uncomfortable on the ears when firing. We experienced feed problems with the AR-18S but, following a logical process of elimination of the possible causes, as laid down by Sandy Cormack, the factory cured the patient.

A bull-pup version of the AR-18 was also produced in prototype form, just to show it could be done. It duly won oohs and aahs from military personnel at exhibitions, and no doubt helped to suggest how attuned the company was to current military thinking. But the prototype did not impress me much, as, like most bull-pups, it offered no real advantage, and it was never taken further. We also produced a run of very smart walnut-stocked AR-180s, which, although they were far too expensive for the American market, did win a few buyers in Europe.

In the meantime, Armalite had involved us in a joint venture to sell a licence for the AR-18 to Chartered Industries of Singapore (CIS). At the time, CIS (which incorporated the Singapore mint) was part of Sheng-Li Holdings, which in turn was wholly owned by the Singapore Government. CIS had purchased a licence from Colt and produced the M-16 very successfully for the Singapore armed forces. They were now anxious to export arms and ammunition, but, under the terms of their Colt agreement, they were not permitted to export the M-16. The AR-18 would therefore have been an ideal follow-on for them to make. Unfortunately they were put off, possibly by Armalite's fee, but more likely by the fact that, since the AR-18 was an American design, American Government approval was needed for every sale.

At the time, CIS was dominated by two men, Ong Kah Kok and Cyril Olson. Ong Kah Kok was the founder and chairman of CIS, a very charming, but very shrewd father figure who was well known around the world, especially as CIS and its sister company, ODE (Ordnance Development and Engineering) had Oerlikon and Bofors licences to manufacture locally. Olson was the general manager, the sole Englishman in a sea of Chinese. A big man in both stature and character, he resembled the TV cop Kojak except that he had a little more hair. He had been an engineer at Shorts, at Chatham on the Medway, and later at Shorts in Belfast. Highly qualified but with very simple, straightforward tastes, he was not easily impressed. He knew what was wanted and he knew how to get it, for he also had the tact, patience and discipline to ensure that the Singaporeans carried it through.

That we came to know and work with CIS is due entirely to David

Howroyd, the Sterling works director. When it was seen that the Armalite deal was foundering, he made the clever suggestion that we might resurrect Frank Waters's 5.56 mm rifle, which had been lying dormant for the past four or five years. An original design, it could easily be picked up again and jointly developed for manufacture in Singapore.

We had decided to patent certain features of the rifle, but, when we had prepared a letter of intent, it was shown in detail to the Singaporeans. Sure enough, as we had half suspected, when the patents were applied for, the British Government attempted to slap a secrecy order on the gun. I should like to say that I think this was done in a spirit of genuine interest in strategic advance, but it might just have been spite. However, as the Singaporeans had already seen the gun, the secrecy order could not stick.

The collaboration with the Singaporeans seemed to be progressing well enough; then everything stopped. I was told to be patient, but nothing at all was happening. It was most frustrating. Then suddenly, out of the blue one day, I was summoned to the Singapore Ministry of Defence, housed in colonial-style buildings near Tanglin Circus. After a short wait I was ushered into a modest but pleasant room to meet Dr Goh Keng Swee, the Minister of Defence and Deputy Prime Minister.

Dr Goh had been at university in Britain, but in the 1950s he probably also spent a spell in prison when the British were trying to stem the tide of nationalism and anti-colonialism. Nevertheless, he gave me a friendly greeting and made me very welcome. Discussing the merits of our project, I found him extremely well informed; and to my satisfaction he gave his whole-hearted approval. After that the effect was like dominoes. Within hours of that meeting, the programme was surging ahead.

The gun emerged as the SAR-80 (the SAR standing for either Sterling Automatic Rifle or Singapore Automatic Rifle). Tooled up in England and made in Singapore, it was a straightforward automatic rifle with gas-operated rotating bolt. It was bought by the Singapore armed forces — and also, I am informed, by the government of Slovenia.

There were several interesting aspects to this collaboration with the Singaporeans. CIS was a comparatively young company, but it had some very highly qualified staff with advanced degrees from various British and Australian universities. At Sterling, apart from my old law degree, there was not a single recognized formal qualification or degree. But Sterling possessed the practical experience that is so necessary in small-arms manufacture. There was also the inevitable oriental preoccupation with 'face'; at all costs, loss of face must be avoided. However, David Howroyd and Frank Waters proved themselves to be consummate diplomats. They never told the Singaporeans how to solve their problems; they merely made suggestions as to how such problems *might* be solved, and allowed the Singaporeans to sort things out for themselves and hence to learn better. The result was a very good working relationship.

There was, however, one joke that we never shared with CIS. When David Howroyd and I had first been shown around CIS, we were impressed by certain aspects of their barrel manufacture (set up by Colt); on returning home, we copied these aspects, with a few minor changes of our own, and so improved our AR-18 barrel production. Then, when the Singaporeans came to Dagenham, armed with cameras and reams of paper on which to take copious notes, we had to hide our amusement when the one area that really interested them was our rifle barrel manufacture.

There was a fair amount of travel during this time, with visits to both Armalite in America and CIS in Singapore. In Singapore I became friendly with Major Adrian Naughten, a Royal Irish Ranger, who was the Assistant Defence Attaché at the British High Commission. After Trinity College, Dublin, he had joined the Army – mainly to prolong his sporting life. He played rugby football for Singapore and was captain of Singapore Cricket Club, and took a great deal of friendly interest in my activities. However, because he was not a member of the Foreign Office he was not invited to social functions; in fact, as far as the High Commission staff were concerned, he was something of a social outcast. I was amazed that so-called diplomats could show such an inflexible attitude.

Sandy Cormack also managed to get himself a design contract in Singapore. He had met the CIS people through Sterling, and was responsible for CIS being able to offer the very best .50″-calibre machine gun available, of the Browning M-2 type, with a dual feed capability.

Armalite had landed me with another possibility for licensed manufacture of their rifle, following an approach made to them involving Saudi money. The Saudis were prepared to fund a non-Eastern Bloc rifle to be produced in its entirety in Egypt, for the benefit (and independence) of the whole Arab world. Egypt was the most advanced of the Arab nations in terms of production engineering, and had already collaborated in the manufacture of various Soviet weapons, including the AK-47 (Kalashnikov) assault rifle. Following a sudden chill in relations between Egypt and the Eastern Bloc in the mid '70s, there was much scurrying around while Western alternatives were sought. So Armalite had been approached, and Armalite in turn had dumped the whole thing on my plate.

I now had to come up with a licence proposal, plus costs, plus a detailed list of plant and tooling needed. Major Keen and I were soon engaged in a series of meetings, mainly with the Saudis and their representatives in London. The interesting part was dealing with the London representatives: two of the best-looking females I had seen in many a long year. They purported to be sisters, or half sisters, but were quite unalike save for the fact that it was hard to judge which was the more beautiful. Paris himself would have got into trouble. Crude male chauvinists that we were, Major Keen and I assumed that this was a bit of a sinecure for the girls, in recognition of past favours carried out somewhere between London and Riyadh. However, so business-like and efficient were they in their approach and organization that I was not even tempted to mix business with pleasure.

Sadly, after a year's intermittent negotiation, the project foundered. The Arabs decided to sink their funds into consumer products instead, and turned their attention towards air-conditioners and ice-makers. I would have given the matter no further thought, except that I started to write a novel based on some of my experiences in the gun business, and wove the two ladies into my plot – indulging my fantasies on paper with shameless elaboration. A publishing friend who read my masterpiece reckoned that the high spot was the part about the two sisters, not that he was impressed by my attempts to write salacious and smutty sex scenes, rather that the 'sisters' were instantly recognizable to him as two women who happened to live in his road. They were not sisters at all, but had had a strong lesbian attachment and had lived together for some time until one went off to get married and the relationship broke up. The arms business is never short of variety.

From time to time during my visits to Armalite's home base in Costa Mesa I had met L. James Sullivan. Jim had worked with Gene Stoner on the AR-15 (M-16) design, and then had gone on to design a series of commercially successful guns and magazines, among them the Mini 14 for Ruger and the Hughes Chain Gun. I had first met him when he was designing for a company called the Red River Company, funded entirely by 'the Duke' himself, none other than John Wayne, who was a genuine gun nut. Jim was determined not to design military guns within America, as Uncle Sam would by law control the export, even if his designs were produced abroad. He did a study for me to build a 5.56 mm Sterling utilizing 60% of the Mark 4's production parts. Frank Waters said it could not be done, but, if I could have afforded Jim, it would have been a most interesting project commercially.

Armalite were instrumental in introducing Jim Sullivan to CIS, where he stayed for three years, designing and developing that quite outstanding 5.56 mm light machine gun with the appalling name: the Ultimax. It made such an impact on me that I secured one for the British Government to test.

Returning to London I contacted the Ministry of Defence and invited them to collect the Ultimax from Sterling for testing, carefully passing on the Singaporeans' particular request that the gun should not be sent to the RSAF at Enfield. (The Singaporeans, aware that the RSAF had a 'rival' gun, were sure the Ultimax would not get an unbiased appraisal.) In due course, the M.O.D. collected the gun and sent it − where else? − to the RSAF at Enfield, where it was submitted to a series of brutal and destructive tests. I never received a test report, in spite of promises that one would be sent, but I understand from my own sources that the gun itself performed well, although pieces of secondary importance (since modified) were broken off. The official attitude seemed to be one of supercilious disbelief that anyone in Singapore could possibly know anything about small-arms.

The fact of the matter is that CIS's Ultimax is light years ahead of Enfield's Light Support Weapon in terms of concept, design and performance, and the progress and dedication of the Singaporeans over recent years has been quite remarkable. Had Britain encouraged private enterprise in this field, rather than undermining it, our developments could have matched those in Singapore, if not exceeded them.

But that was no isolated incident.

There was a time when the ammunition factory, ROF Radway Green, near Crewe, was out of action, unable to produce 9 mm Parabellum ammunition. I was keen to produce this calibre and went to the M.O.D. with a scheme to install a plant if they would only order a batch of 15 million rounds per year from me. In production terms this was a tiny amount − but it was too much for the M.O.D. to swallow. They could not oblige us, they said, because of the Preferred Source Policy (again); and anyway, Radway would soon be up and running again, able to meet the demand. But in the meantime, as we knew, the M.O.D. was in trouble. We were receiving complaints from units in Northern Ireland that guns (L2A3s) were misfeeding, and thereby endangering the lives of serving British soldiers. (If they had had the Sterling, with a different chamber, this would not have happened.) The problem was caused by the ammunition − 9 mm Parabellum, but made essentially for pistols − which the M.O.D. had been forced to buy in from France, Pakistan, India and Australia. It was, in fact, the M.O.D.'s own Preferred Source Policy that was endangering the lives of serving British soldiers.

It still amazes me that the M.O.D. should have been so determined to stifle competition within the UK that it went overseas to supplement its needs. Apart from anything else, it seems that balance of payments was not a consideration.

Even today, I wonder whether anyone in power ever thought through the consequences of their actions. If you stifle competition, the competition dies. You then have the field to yourself, but without competition you grow weak and slow. When the need arises you cannot fulfil it, and so you must go cap in hand to foreign rivals. And meanwhile there is the cost; the cost of supporting those whom you have put out of business, and the cost of buying in what you need from elsewhere, and the human

cost as well − including low morale within your own industry.
And I'm sure the same could be said about other fields than gun manufacture.

CHAPTER TWELVE

Into Civvy Street

Yaffle, the civilian gun distribution company that we had acquired in 1975, was now being run by Tom Kent. Formerly a driver at Sterling, he was unswayed by the emotion of guns; he ran the business carefully and dispassionately, consolidating its successes and slowly improving its turnover and profits. As a result, Sterling was now better placed to judge this market and we began to consider making a new product: an airgun.

The idea was to try and bridge the gap between civilian and military guns, and airguns seemed to be one of the most obvious options. Simple guns, operated by compressed air, they could with relatively little effort acquire a military relevance − in training, for example.

One of several possibilities that we examined came through Tony Bianco. A young Royal Artillery major who looked more Sicilian than British, Tony had joined Sterling as a back-up for Major Keen. He had been in close touch with RFD (the company named after Reginald Foster Dagnall, born 1880) of Godalming, who had made certain advances in the use of small-arms for simulated training in the police and the military. Of particular interest to us was a pre-charged air cartridge that could be used in a normal gun; when fired it would discharge an airgun pellet. It was the brainchild of an automotive engineer called Michael Saxby. In practical terms, the air stored in the cartridge was always subject to too many variable conditions, which could affect accuracy, but in the revolver role it showed great promise. Anyway, it was Mike Saxby himself who approached Sterling with a proposal that we should make an air rifle based on his patents.

It would certainly have been easy enough to make. However, by this time Yaffle was employing a gun expert by the name of Brett Parsons; he had been with Parker Hale, the famous Birmingham manufacturers of sporting guns, and he knew the civilian market well. Although I liked the product, Brett Parsons did not. He felt that airgunners would soon get bored with the hassle of having to pre-charge their plastic rounds by pumping air into them. In fact, he was adamant that we should not go ahead, and we bowed to his expert advice. I was glad that we did. Saxby later went ahead with his idea and produced a Saxby & Palmer rifle (coincidentally working with Parker Hale). It caused an initial flurry of enthusiasm in the market, then all but died.

Another approach to Sterling was from John Whiscombe, a computer expert with an interest in airguns and a clear understanding of trends in airgun developments. He had cleverly adapted the German GISS system — a spring recoilless system — for an airgun, although he was adrift on the cost of manufacture. But it was felt that this was too sophisticated for Sterling to make as a first-off airgun, and it would be too expensive for the market that we were aiming at. We devoted more time to consideration of a design put forward by two personable engineers, David Theobald and Ben Taylor, who had formed the Theoben Company in Huntingdon. However, their idea involved a barrel-cocking airgun and when we consulted the gun trade we found them unanimously of the opinion that barrel-cocking airguns were on the way out. I have since learned to pay less heed to what the gun trade says. Too many people can list their likes and dislikes, particularly the latter; but, when it comes to buying a product that they themselves have encouraged, they rarely put their money where their mouth is.

But we finally found what we were looking for. Roy Hutchinson, an airgun enthusiast and designer who had his own engineering facility, had designed a powerful underlever cocking spring gun. The main feature of his design was the power of the gun, and the fact that a small bolt was used to push the pellet into the barrel. This ensured that the skirt of the pellet was in no way deformed, so that there was a perfect seal in the rifling and hence no loss of power. Sterling had the machining capacity and the tooling was made in-house. Responsibility for the whole project was given to a young engineer called Peter Moon, whose production background had been in the frantic world of domestic appliances and progress was rapid. There was a bit of a rub when Roy took his time over producing drawings, so Peter designed his own solution to the problem. The result was the HR-81 rifle. It was downright ugly, on account of the engineer's cosmetics and the very cheap Italian stock. More important, though, it was particularly well made, powerful and effective, and it has already become a classic, much sought after.

The trade told me confidently that the new rifle would never sell; it used an underlever, and underlevers were things of the past. For a while, the trade seemed to be right. The rifle did not sell at first, and I became quite worried. Suddenly, however, it caught on and we were in the happy position of being able to sell all that we could make. Furthermore, it spawned a fashion in airguns, so that the underlever came back with a vengeance; it is now more popular than the sidelever.

As the HR-81 was something entirely new, we offered a no-quibble guarantee that we would replace any gun returned for any reason at all. A handful came back with scratched or damaged stocks, and were instantly replaced, although the damage must have occurred after the guns were despatched from Sterling. Others came back to us in pieces, because some know-all had been going to tune his gun to produce yet more power. Since the rifle was assembled with the mainspring held under considerable pressure, in a special press, these amateur would-be tuners did not stand a chance of getting the pieces back together again. Still, for the sake of improving the name and keeping the customers happy, we reassembled the guns for free. This service was even extended to those who claimed that they had barely removed the weapon from its original packing and certainly never even fired it — but we would find burred screw heads and scratches, the tell-tale signs that a 'tinker' had been at work. Without comment, we would reassemble or replace the particular weapon. The trade, without saying too much themselves, appreciated these gestures, and the business began to snowball.

Perhaps it is not just orientals who regard loss of face as all-important.

Another option that we were considering was handguns. Among the companies Yaffle represented was the Italian firm of Benelli, makers of one of the world's best automatic shotguns, who had come up with an exciting new design. A good-looking pistol, it was made in a most interesting way, in that the main frame consisted of two pressings plasma-welded together (the weld was impossible to detect). Paolo Benelli's enthusiasm was infectious and we ended up importing some for the English home market; however, though selling well enough, they failed to make the impact we were looking for.

At the time, the police were mainly interested in the good old six-shot revolver (this was as true of the Americans as it was of the British). The revolver was simply regarded as more reliable than the self-loading pistol. It may have been partly a hangover from the incident in 1974 when Princess Anne was attacked in the Mall and her bodyguard's Walther pistol jammed. Webley & Scott had discontinued revolver manufacture with a simple .38″ some years before, and the round required had jumped from .38″ Special to .357″ Magnum. Even the French police were thinking about switching to revolvers, and Manurhin (Manufacture de Machines du Haut-Rhin), who at one stage made Walther guns under licence, had just launched quite a good .357″ Magnum revolver.

In short, the handgun market was somewhat confusing. We needed an adviser, and the obvious man for the job was Don Mitchell, who at one stage in his career had headed up handgun sales at Colt. He was quick to point out that if we went in for handguns we would be facing some very stiff competition from the well-established American firms. He also stressed that a high manufacturing standard and an even higher standard of finish were essential. Cosmetics are everything! Then, settling to the task, he told us how he'd had dealings with an American firm called Hawes, who had bought in a very tidy revolver from the old-established German company of J. P. Sauer & Sohn GmbH of Eckenfoerde. He had had experience of that company before, because Colt used to buy all their hunting rifles from Sauer, and the quality was very high. However, the arrangement had ended as the prices out of Germany made the rifles quite uncompetitive on the American market. Now Don Mitchell was suggesting that I should contact the head of the firm, Dr Rolf Murmann, and I duly did so.

Dr Murmann was one of the old-fashioned Prussian military

types, lacking only the *pickelhaube*, and he proved very friendly. Invited to visit Eckenfoerde, which is north of the Kiel Canal in the far north of what used to be West Germany, I was shown their .38″ Special revolver. It was well made and well finished, but its unique feature was a totally compensated trigger pull; that is, the pressure that had to be exerted on the trigger itself during the firing cycle remained absolutely constant. Sauer realized, however, that to stay in the market they needed to produce a gun that could take .357″ Magnum, which would involve both a major redesign and further investment. Meanwhile they had dived back into the pistol market and had set up to manufacture the new SIG pistols. It was a good partnership; having the pistols manufactured in Germany meant that the Swiss could export them universally. Both parties were German-speaking, and Sauer's smart new factory and reputation for quality only underlined that of SIG with their excellent new range of pistols. Eventually SIG bought the Murmanns out, and Sauer is now a wholly owned subsidiary of SIG.

Sauer had already sold the existing .38″ Special revolver to Armi San Paulo in Italy, who planned to carry on making it just as before, hoping that the lower Italian labour rates would allow them to recapture a share of the market through more competitive prices. This did not worry me unduly as we wanted a more powerful revolver and intended to tool it up properly for our own factory.

I did, however, secure a deal with Sauer on the trigger patent. We also acquired a loan of the drawings of the old revolver, which would save Frank Waters a lot of time in the drawing up of a new .357″ Magnum revolver. Within 18 months, Sterling had produced 20 pre-production revolvers.

On display at a shot show and at the International Hunting Show at Nuremburg, the revolvers aroused no little interest. In fact, even the mighty Smith & Wesson were so impressed that they copied our new look, extending the ejection-rod shroud in silhouette to the end of the barrel and thus producing a chunkier and more business-like and aggressive appearance.

Most notable among those who showed interest was Norinco, from the People's Republic of China. A party of 20 Chinese visited Sterling to inspect the revolver and its drawings. They were clearly very taken with the gun, though I think our master-stroke was a buffet laid on in the offices by the secretaries and the local Chinese takeaway. Slowly we progressed towards a deal. My idea was to give Norinco a free licence for all production, but for Sterling to retain exclusive rights over sales in every country other than China. But this was all happening at the time when I was about to sell Sterling. Unfortunately, the new owners in their wisdom started talking to the Chinese about licence fees, and the whole deal sank into oblivion.

I'm still convinced that our Sterling revolvers could have made powerful inroads in the American market. They fired beautifully.

The only other product about which we were serious was Armalite's AR-17 aluminium shotgun: they called it 'the Golden Gun'. It was a two-shot automatic using a recoil-operated multi-lug rotating bolt for locking the system. The barrel and the body were made out of aluminium, and the furniture was made of polycarbonate plastic. The gun weighed under six pounds, had a selection of screw-on chokes (to reduce bore size) and was, in shooting terminology, a sheer joy to point. (When one swings a shotgun to shoot a bird in flight, with a movement rather like the stroke of a paint-brush, one is 'pointing'; because the AR-17 was so light, it had exceptional 'pointability'.) It looked appalling, but nothing that black (as opposed to gold) anodizing and wooden furniture could not cure. More to the point, we were sceptical about the aluminium standing up to the loads and pressures. We therefore commissioned a 20,000-round test from Nils Ruder and Carl Perrson of Singlepoint, Bob Jennings' old firm. In the meantime we asked Moog Hydra-point, an Anglo-American machine-tool manufacturer, to make some studies for the machining of the aluminium receiver on one of their light-machining centres.

Singlepoint did a wonderful job, testing and reporting and even carrying out running repairs. The overall conclusion, in simple terms, was that the aluminium barrel and receiver performed faultlessly, but the rest of the gun did not last so well. Odd parts became fatigued and broke. However, they were all capable of remedy.

It was for quite separate reasons that the project had to be abandoned. We realized that we needed some specialist expertise in setting the impact extrusions of the body and the barrel; two different sorts of forging experts were needed and we could only find one. Furthermore, the latter pitched his fees so high that it overbalanced the deal. It was no consolation, but I think he imagined we were such a successful company that we could afford to pay the earth.

Another idea that fell by the wayside came from Sandy Cormack. When he heard that I was looking at Brocks, and then Astra, he had started designing a riot gun cum signal pistol. It was actually reduced to engineering drawings for production by a young Singaporean student from CIS who was spending his long vacation with Sterling. It had some very neat features, but at the time there was no spare administrative capacity to put it into production.

More of a near miss was a Sterling sniper rifle. Tony Bianco attached great importance to maximizing the sales on high-value accessories, and successfully sold Pilkington night-vision equipment. However, a sniper rifle with specialist add-ons would be less price-sensitive, as there is a degree of bespoke tailoring on each order. The trouble was that the world abounds with good-quality hunting rifles; we would need something very special.

I approached Alf Scott, the then managing director of BSA Guns Ltd in Birmingham, and asked if they could produce a sniper rifle exclusively for Sterling. It was not such a big operation, since they only had to combine the features of their 7.62 mm target rifle with a 7.62 mm hunting rifle. They agreed, and a small number of the BSA/Sterling sniper rifles were duly produced, then combined with the valuable accessories and sold. However, during one demonstration in the Arabian Gulf area, on which we had pinned high hopes for a decent sale, we discovered that something was radically wrong. The BSA/Sterling sniper rifle was, obviously, meant to be highly accurate; however, at distances of only 200 yards it produced results no better than a standard Sterling sub-machine gun without a telescopic sight.

On a hunch, I rang Ken White, the then works manager at BSA. He was audibly annoyed at the suggestion that anything might be wrong at the BSA end of the operation. But one simple question revealed the truth. I asked him what sort of barrel the rifle had: whether it was 7.62 mm, or .308″ Winchester (the American calibre, developed by the Winchester rifle company, that is the exact equivalent to 7.62 mm), or .30-06″. The latter is very marginally different; .30-06″ rounds can be fired from a 7.62 mm gun, but there is inevitably a loss of accuracy.

He said: 'Is there any difference?'

Unsurprisingly, we did not win the sniper rifle contract for the country concerned. It was not worthwhile tooling up for our own sniping rifle as the quantities required were minimal. Sauer had a beautiful sniper rifle, and so did Mauser, but only at enormous cost. It seemed to us improbable that the product would ever be more than a prestigious loss-leader.

Just at that time, however, the M.O.D. invited tenders for a new sniper rifle, with a quantity of a thousand to be awarded for the first order. All the top British firms were eager candidates for this honour — Parker-Hale, Interarms and Edgcumbe Arms. And I discovered that someone else was keen to enter the contest. Malcolm Cooper, the British shooting gold medallist at numerous Olympics, had built a prototype with some interesting features and was looking for a manufacturer. It seemed like a good marriage. Alas, Sterling became involved in other troubles which meant that we never made it to the altar. The sad irony is that, although Malcolm Cooper won the trial, he had to use engineering sub-contractors whose skills did not match his own. Even among those manufacturers who have experience of firearms, there is a tendency to underrate the need for high precision and accuracy. The M.O.D. were satisifed with the results, but the manufacturer encountered an inordinate degree of difficulty in making the gun, and Malcolm Cooper himself was reportedly very disappointed.

CHAPTER THIRTEEN

Brits in Knots

Travel broadens the mind, they say, but it also builds up the business. Apart from the two grand tours I made early on, to the Far East and to South America, I made many shorter trips to many different countries, seldom staying anywhere for more than 48 hours. It was often wearying; it was also very necessary. Usually there were specific objectives – chasing a deal, sorting out a problem, signing a contract – but sometimes it was necessary merely in order to keep up the momentum, to make sure the customers were happy or simply to keep the company name in people's minds. Furthermore, Major Keen and Major Bianco were also travelling; when Beavan Keen's health broke down, Tony Bianco willingly undertook yet more travel. He enjoyed covering the Arabian Gulf area while I tended to do the Far East, especially the regular visits to Chartered Industries of Singapore.

But one of the hazards of travel, particularly in the arms business, is the necessary dependence on people whose motives are not always clear. There was one deal that gave us considerable aggravation, and all because of one man.

It was Tony Bianco who managed to secure the order from the Kuwaiti Ministry of Defence for a quantity of Mark 5 silenced guns and 150 Pilkington night-vision scopes. The Mark 5s could be supplied from stock, but Pilkington had to make up the scopes. For reasons of cash flow, we agreed to supply the guns immediately but to send the night-sights and mounts separately over the next three months. The Mark 5s duly went off, along with detailed instructions on how to disassemble them and fit the night-sight mounts when they arrived, and with two separate armourer's kits, whose main items were an alignment gauge and special torque spanners. Tony Bianco himself went over the details of how to reassemble the guns. Short of going out there ourselves to do the job, there was nothing more we could do.

Some time later, word reached us through the British military attaché that the Kuwaitis were dissatisfied with the guns. The specific complaint was that they were inaccurate. Not one or two, but all of them.

We found this hard to believe. Although it had never been heard of before at Sterling, there might just have been one rogue gun. But 150 was just downright impossible. Every weapon that left Sterling was comprehensively tested. Probing gently, we were assured that the problem was definitely the guns themselves; they had been examined and assembled by a specialist armourer from the Kuwait Liaison Team (British soldiers who acted in an advisory capacity to the Kuwaiti armed forces), and he had pronounced them 'all wrong'.

David Howroyd took this assurance at face value. He had the whole consignment of guns flown back to England. When they arrived at Dagenham, we found that only a handful had ever been removed from their original packing. Four or five guns had been opened, fitted with the Pilkington mounts and reassembled. But it was immediately clear that the work had been done without regard either to the armourer's kit or to the instructions. The torque spanners and alignment gauges had not been used, and the silencing arrangements were all out of alignment, since the tie rods had been over-tightened.

Within twenty-four hours at Sterling, all 150 guns had been fitted, reassembled and despatched once more to the customer. We were left wondering which of two possible explanations was right. The more charitable explanation was that some British soldier had been either too slothful or too conceited to bother to read the instructions; perhaps he thought he was an experienced armourer and could thus dispense with such a chore, or perhaps he found it beneath his dignity. The other possibility was deliberate commercial sabotage. We already knew that Heckler & Koch's British friends were trying to push the Gulf countries into buying the silenced version of the H & K MP-5. It would have been all too easy for them to subvert Sterling's efforts in the Gulf.

On the whole, however, people tended to be remarkably helpful and supportive. In fact, those at the top were usually only too keen to assist.

As I've mentioned, the company had been successful in selling Mark 5s to the Argentinian naval commandos. The odd thing was that the Argentinians made their own sub-machine guns, the Halcon and the PAM, but the military factories were run by the Army and the Navy did not trust the quality of their products. This was partly a symptom of the inter-service rivalry, but also an understandable precaution when terrorist activity and sabotage were so widespread throughout Argentina. For the same reason, although they made their own 9 mm ammunition, they also bought in foreign supplies. I even arranged one sale to the Argentinians of a quantity of 9 mm Parabellum ammunition made by the Royal Ordnance Factory, Radway Green.

Then, in 1980, I received an order from Argentina for a quantity of Mark 4s. We applied in the usual way for an export licence, but to our surprise the Department of Trade and Industry turned us down. The surprise turned to indignation when I read in *The Times* one day that the Industry Secretary − then Cecil Parkinson − was about to visit Argentina with the specific aim of promoting Anglo-Argentinian business. They were funding one of their own number to visit Argentina and seek further business and orders for British industry, yet they declined to issue me with an export licence. The D.T.I. were never obliged to give reasons for any refusal, but it was well known that they sought advice from the Foreign and Commonwealth Office and we had assumed, in this case, that the word had gone out: Argentina is a contentious area, stop all export licences. Yet now it appeared that we had assumed wrong. I simply could not understand it, so I telephoned Cecil Parkinson and asked to see him. He very kindly consented to a meeting just before he was due to leave.

The meeting was held at the D.T.I. in Victoria Street, London, on 6 November 1980. Tony Bianco was with me. Cecil Parkinson took the chair. The others comprised repesentatives from the Export Licensing Branch of the D.T.I., from M.O.D. Sales and from the Foreign and Commonwealth Office. After I had said my little piece, the Foreign Office man had his turn. There was absolutely no prospect of Sterling being granted an export licence, he stated grimly, and he was not at liberty to say why, beyond mentioning a dispute with Argentina over the Falkland Islands.

Cecil Parkinson smiled at me wryly. He had given me a chance to put my case directly; but that was all he could do. Even if he could grant me the export licence, he said, his successor would be sure to rescind it 'within 48 hours'.

That was that.

We never did get that export licence; nor did we find out exactly why. However, in April 1982, less than 18 months after our meeting at the D.T.I. when the Foreign Office were being accused of negligence in their dealings with the Argentine Government, I was astounded to hear their assertion that the invasion of the Falkland Islands had been entirely unexpected.

Half the problem, in the arms business certainly, is knowing whom to trust. After a while one learns to be wary; not everyone is what he seems. In London, as elsewhere, there are many 'Mr Fixits' who are only too ready to help. They all run a smart office with rubber plants, a well-spoken secretary and a second-hand Rolls-Royce. They may even have had some modicum of success due to an ephemeral contact. During the 1970s and early '80s the great game was to secure advance deposits from the hopeful buyer; although guaranteed to be returned if the sale should fall through, the deposits inevitably netted a huge interest for the individual concerned. Sometimes the goods existed, high-value new or second-hand military equipment, perhaps. Sometimes they were mere figments of the imagination.

The trouble was that these characters often seemed so plausible. One was even introduced to me by an old college friend from Oxford, a one-time M.P. The man my friend introduced to me was Greek, a self-styled Mr Fixit of the arms world, whom I shall call Spyros Eustathiades (I've changed his name so as to protect those who may still be trying to salvage contractual arrangements with him).

Eustathiades was very presentable, warm, smiling and open. He gave the impression of great wealth in the way he dressed and in the continual references to his yacht in Greece and to his penthouse suite on top of one of London's better hotels. The natural assumption is that some sort of success is paying the bills. He had marvellous contacts, he told me − chiefs of staff of this country and that, ministers of defence, everyone had apparently been entertained by Eustathiades on board his yacht. He could virtually guarantee me a huge jump in sales. The only condition was that we should grant him the sole, exclusive rights to sell Sterling's products all over the world.

That first meeting ended with my agreeing to visit him in his penthouse suite. As further bait, I was invited to go to Greece as his guest and spend a week on his yacht.

The suite turned out to be comfortable but small, just two rooms, something well short of the picture he had conveyed. But he had telephone and telex, and access to secretarial services, as and when he needed them. He also had the prestige of a magnificent address without having to lash out on buying a place of his own, or going to all the expense of staffing and running an office in central London. I rather admired him; it was certainly one better than running a business from a serviced box number.

However, I already had my doubts about Eustathiades. As he continued his patter, reeling off the names of all the grand and great with whom he had hobnobbed on yachts in the Mediterranean, I laid a little trap. I happened to have an acquaintance, a member of one reasonably well-known family, who quite definitely did not have a yacht in Greece − and Eustathiades apparently knew them and their yacht intimately. I told him that I was quite prepared to discuss some kind of sales arrangement but he would have to bring some business to the table first. This was a not unreasonable request, given that the company had already made sales of varying quantities in some hundred countries. It was probably my imagination, but I thought I saw the hope dying in his eyes.

· The next morning I rang Cyril Olson at Chartered Industries in Singapore, to ask if he had heard of the great Eustathiades. Over the phone came a very rude word. Cyril told me that the man was a complete waste of time; he had involved CIS in countless quotations, none of them ever bearing fruit. He pleaded with me not to have anything to do with the man.

Needless to say, I heard no more from Mr Spyros Eustathiades. I reported the facts back to my friend, who was a little embarrassed at having been taken in, though I'm sure he was not the only one to be conned. The whole art of the confidence trickster is to play on what people want to believe. In the arms business, we're all looking for the man who can turn talk into orders. They do exist, I'm told. Sterling being the success it was, we attracted all sorts of attention, some more welcome than others, from people who wanted to share the cake.

In Hong Kong, for example, we were represented by the aptly named Roger Gunn of Jardine Mathieson. Jardines were especially keen to be our agents in Indonesia and the Philippines, but we already had a long-standing commitment to agents there. However, in spite of the fact that there was virtually no market for our sub-machine guns in Hong Kong, we had another credible contestant for representation there and in certain other local territories. Simon Murray was an ex-soldier who knew the qualities of the Sterling and was desperately keen to win the agency, if only for reasons of status. In fact his persistence paid off and he did later become Sterling's agent, but he soon graduated into very much more profitable pursuits. He has written an excellent book about his military exploits, which included a spell in the French Foreign Legion (where he rose to the rank of sergeant, almost the top rank if you are not a Frenchman). His experience of sub-machine guns was limited to the ugly and very heavy MAT-49; it actually works reasonably well within its limitations but the Sterling is altogether in a different class. This latter-day Beau Geste then sought his fortune in Hong Kong where, ironically, he worked for Jardines before leaving to form his own company, Davenham Investments. Today he runs Hutchisons Whampoa as the right-hand man of Lee Ka Shung, thereby holding one of the top jobs in Hong Kong.

Sterling also attracted attention in some quarters merely because it was an armaments manufacturing company. Even within the arms business, there are some deluded people who see it as glamorous, alluring and intrinsically exciting, and outsiders tend to fall neatly into one of two camps: those who regard anything to do with armaments as morally indefensible and those who are fascinated. The former generally grow out of it; the latter are always with us. If I hadn't realized this before, it was certainly brought home to me in May 1982.

A friend of mine, Peter Dineley, who owns and runs the arms and militaria hire firm of Bapty & Co (and also a company called Kensington Gore which specializes in theatrical blood), had been the first person to apply to be a passenger on the newly re-created Orient Express − properly called the 'Venice-Simplon-Orient Express' − as launched by Jim Sherwood of Sea Containers Ltd. Peter was asked to make up a party of four, and so he and I and our respective wives made the historic trip to Venice, dressed as 1930s lounge lizards, in the company of Jim Sherwood, of course, and his English wife Shirley and many well-known or affluent personalities such as Liza Minelli, Jeffrey (now Lord) Sterling of P & O fame, the Marquess of Bristol and many others whose names are better dropped by Nigel Dempster of the *Daily Mail* (who was also on board). Valerie Kleeman and Alan Whicker had also come along for the ride, to make a 'Whicker's World' programme of the trip. His interview technique fascinated me; he apparently just made a few genial remarks, then sat back to listen to all that the interviewee said in response.

My trouble was that I was so busy enjoying the gastronomy (thanks to Pru Leith), bonhomie and free-flowing champagne that I completely failed to rise to the occasion. Alan Whicker, out for fun, was trying to hype things up a bit, to such an extent that we fully expected a 'murder'; and he talked mysteriously about some great arms dealer who was on the train. I couldn't think who he meant. Obviously neither Peter nor myself could fit the bill. Later, however, I got it in the neck from my wife. He *had* meant me. He had been offering me a chance to ham it up as a second Basil Zaharoff, the Turkish arms dealer whose activities won him widespread fame and influence. Oblivious as usual to the way others perceived my occupation, I had missed my own big moment.

Undoubtedly the greatest Mr Fixit of modern times in Adnan Kashoggi. His organization is unparalleled; it is rumoured that they even have their own satellite communications. I did have contact with his organization, Triad, but since I was already doing business in those areas where they were strongest, there would be no great benefit from Sterling's point of view and anyway it would have been very small beer for them.

From the greatest to lowest, all arms dealers share the same motivation: making money. In this they are no different from other businessmen, but somehow they have acquired a reputation for being uniquely unprincipled, which is probably not wholly fair, or not, at least, in all cases. What most bothered me about many of the Mr Fixits I encountered was that they always preferred to lever a situation by barter rather than outright sale. My problem was that I always had to pay a labour force in hard British currency so that their wives could shop at Tesco on a Friday afternoon. As a result, I often had to turn down some very tempting offers: cigars, for instance (I was very keen to do a deal here); Marlboro cigarettes made in Bulgaria; South African sparkling wine; Haitian rum; frozen shellfish; counterfeit American dollars at 50% of their face value (they would have passed muster only in a darkened room) – and, yes, drugs. Had I succumbed to temptation, I could undoubtedly have made a fortune several times over, but I preferred to keep my conscience clean.

At least the dealers are prepared to admit their motivation more or less openly. Governments, on the other hand, tend to be more hypocritical, mouthing platitudes about morality while at the same time seeking out the dealers to do business. Arms manufacturers are to some degree relieved of moral responsibility in that they are obliged to secure government export licences. The fact is, however, that most governments are only too eager to grant export licences; defence equipment is big business and employs many people, and though the political risks are high the potential benefits are generally thought worthwhile. (Incidentally, in Britain it is sometimes said that, when the Labour Party is in power, export licences must be harder to come by, yet the opposite is true; they are marginally easier to obtain, perhaps because the Civil Service has more opportunity to flex its muscles independently.)

Precisely because of these potential gains, there is world-wide overproduction of arms. Once a given country has satisfied the domestic needs of her own armed forces, then she can afford to offer competitive supply to friendly foreign countries. Not only does this produce tangible profit, it also cements relations between countries, sometimes even leading to one country becoming reliant on another. In other words, arms sales can be used as an instrument of foreign policy

It is no moral argument to state that 'if we don't supply then someone else will'; but this is often no more and no less than the truth. While the rest of the world ostracized Libya, for instance, Brazil stepped in to supply armoured vehicles and small-arms, and thus gave a boost to her own fledgling arms industry. Yet there is, broadly speaking, at least a degree of international agreement over the real moral arguments. Any country with obvious human rights problems must not receive equipment that will aggravate the situation (such as Chile and South Africa). Any country that sympathizes openly with terrorist organizations (such as Libya) must not be supplied. Any country that might turn our own equipment on us should not be supplied — but this is a tricky one; it is impossible to forecast who might be so unsporting (such as Argentina and Iraq).

Somehow France is an exception to the prevailing rules. The French are probably the most sanguine over arms sales, and yet have not suffered any excess of criticism. The rest of us in the West seem to have cyclical bouts of moral hand-wringing over whom we sell arms to and when. However, a refusal to supply arms can sometimes be even more damaging in the long run. Countries like Israel, South Africa and Chile, which for one reason or another are proscribed, naturally feel a need to ensure continuity of supplies and therefore make the decision to develop their own arms industries; then, once these are up and running, they usually exceed demand at home and go into surplus. It is well known, for instance, that in the Gulf War of 1991, South African T-5s were among the best artillery pieces in the Iraqi Army, and some of their other advanced equipment (British-designed) came from Cardoen in Chile.

As always, during a time of surplus the dealers turn out to be the chief beneficiaries. Courted by manufacturers, cultivated by governments, they invariably scoop the cream off any profits. But if the dealers sometimes deserve censure, they are not the only ones.

During the Second World War, my godfather, who built steering gears for ships (John Hastie & Co of Greenock, Scotland), used to fly to Stockholm to buy ball bearings. He would find himself being entertained alongside officers of the German High Command, buying the same articles. Sweden was neutral, of course. Like the Swiss, the Swedes appear to have an innate urge to maintain their neutrality, possibly for financial reasons as much as for moral ones. Certainly they have benefited by not having had to partake in successive world wars. Nevertheless, building fine equipment to maintain a balance of power is one thing; war profiteering is another.

The constitutions of both Sweden and Switzerland prevent the export of arms except in certain circumstances. However, there is nothing to prevent a Swedish or Swiss arms company from setting up outside the national boundaries, either in their own factory or by licensing agreement. Only the Swedes and the Swiss themselves appeared to be surprised at the rumpus that ensued when it was discovered, in the mid 1980s, that Singaporean licensees of both Bofors and Oerlikon were supplying arms and ammunition to Iraq. As in so many things, the great crime is getting found out.

I was once approached by an Irishman who had apparently conducted business in various parts of the world for United Scientific Instruments, one of Britain's leading manufacturers of military instruments and sights. While talking about his experience in certain countries, he casually mentioned the way it was sometimes necessary to bend the rules slightly. I listened but made no reaction, which seemed vaguely to disappoint him. Later I had him checked out but unusually did not hear the result of the investigation. I do know that he was not apprehended, for we spoke again, although he showed no further interest in the particular line he had been pursuing. It then occurred to me that this had been a little test, set by the British authorities, to see how I would respond. The Irishman, in fact, had probably been a plant.

CHAPTER FOURTEEN

Africa Adieu

South Africa seems to me to be, of all countries, the object of the greatest posturing and cant. Other countries have worse records in the field of human rights, yet escape the world's opprobium. Nevertheless, when the United Nations Security Council first imposed a voluntary arms embargo against South Africa in 1963 (it became mandatory in 1977), it was an attempt to express the international abhorrence of apartheid.

Up till then, the position in Britain was that the Government would probably have sold arms to South Africa, as a bulwark against Communism; that is, strategic military equipment was sold so long as it could not be used to enforce the policy of apartheid. The sale of a submarine would probably have been allowed, and the principle might well have been extended to Buccaneer and maritime reconnaissance aircraft, but armoured vehicles and small-arms were certainly in the forbidden category.

However, even when there is a ban on the sale of arms to a particular country, if that country has already bought equipment then it is easier to sell spare parts without raising so many eyebrows. The ban is evaded by selling the spares, often through a dealer, to some third country. On occasion, the sale is ostensibly made to other countries in Southern Africa that are effectively South African dependencies. In fact, South Africa has had overt support from Iran (in Imperial days), Israel, France, Italy and Britain. More covert assistance has come from several countries in both Western and Eastern Europe (in particular Spain), as well as from Jordan, some Caribbean territories and the USA.

In 1977 I visited a gunshop in Cape Town, A. Rosenthal (Cape)

(Pty) Ltd of Long Market Street, which was extremely well stocked. The proprietor, a German south-wester by the name of Bryan Smit, showed me round with pride. I saw American, German, Austrian, Italian and Spanish rifles and pistols, and Swedish ammunition. They also had South African rifles made up from Mauser actions dating from the Second World War, on to which they put Swedish Bofors barrels and their own stocks. They had one English rifle, a Parker Hale; it was the only item in the whole shop that had been bought indirectly. Equally revealing was a visit to the Uhersky Brod factory of Brno in Czechoslovakia, where they were making the CZ-75 pistol and excellent bolt-action hunting rifles; they were executing an order for 20,000 pieces for Botswana.

Under the international ban, even sporting guns are prohibited, and yet South Africa is awash with guns.

The absurdity of it all is pointed up by an incident that occurred in the early '80s. Two gentlemen that I know quite well, and with whom I had done business in the past, were charged with contravening Customs and Excise regulations: they had tried to despatch spare parts for the M-2 Browning machine gun to South Africa. They were convicted and sentenced to jail. I visited one of them in Grendon Underwood open prison near Aylesbury. He was fit and well; the regime did him more good than a health farm. But it seemed wrong to me that an elderly engineer should have to 'do bird'. He and his colleague had not tried to cheat anybody financially; they had tried to operate in what they considered to be the interests of the free world. They were misguided and foolish, not dishonest. They were also small fry, unable to hit back; perhaps that was why they were dealt with so savagely. *Pour encourager les autres.*

My in-laws farmed in the northern Transvaal in South Africa. We would manage Christmas with them most years, and at the end of the holiday we would sneak a few extra days when I could go customer-calling.

I made it very clear, when I first contacted the Armaments Board in Pretoria in 1974, that it was against international law to sell arms to South Africa and I had no intention of breaking the law. However, friends are always welcome, and, hopefully, some of South Africa's problems will be sorted out in the near future. My approach was purely for interest's sake.

I had already been in touch with J. Neethling Coetzee who was with the Armaments Board in Pretoria. He had been involved with BSA in the 1960s. At that time, BSA had been making the self-loading rifle for the British Government; when a tender went out for a further tranche, the RSAF at Enfield quoted a price 18% above the one offered by BSA. However, as the RSAF was a government entity, not even a nationalized industry, they were automatically awarded the further contract (under the Preferred Source Policy). The directors of BSA were so disgusted that they vowed the company would have nothing more to do with military small-arms, after nearly a century of involvement. The South Africans were in the course of negotiating a licence agreement with FN in Belgium to manufacture the FAL (Fusil automatique légère), which is virtually the same as the SLR. The story goes that FN expected to make the bulk of their profit on the supply of plant, equipment and tooling. However, BSA sold their complete line to the South African Government. What is true is that one of the best versions of the SLR/FAL was made in South Africa. Again, it may be apocryphal, but BSA's equipment and tooling were supposedly given imperial measurements, and the FN drawings were in metric: the conversion apparently caused the South Africans a great deal of expense.

In 1976 I was in South Africa some time after the Russians had brought out the AK-74, their small-calibre version of the Avtomat Kalashnikova 47 rifle. The British Government and others had been besieging me for information on this new weapon; nobody in the West had been able to get hold of one. I mentioned the new AK-74 to Neethling Coetzee, and he grinned, beckoning me into a laboratory. There he showed me the rounds, drawings of the ammunition and the new barrels, and detailed information about every new aspect of the weapon. He explained that a group of South Africans had been invited to Hungary. This amazed me, for I knew what the Hungarians thought of South Africa. Once, when I had been planning to buy some Hungarian machine tools, the Commercial Attaché at the Hungarian Embassy in London had invited my wife and me to a New Year's Eve party in Budapest. When I told him that my wife still had a South African passport, he said that they would not let her in; he begged me to get her a British passport, but unfortunately there wasn't enough time. So I looked at Neethling Coetzee in astonishment. He and his colleagues were all Afrikaners, with very obviously Afrikaans names; they couldn't possibly have had British passports. Or could they? Neethling smiled again, nodding in the affirmative. All I can deduce is that the Brits and the South Africans were and are a lot closer than they would have the rest of the world believe.

My relationship with the South Africans very nearly bore financial fruit. One of the most successful weapons of all time was the pre-war, Czech-designed, light machine gun built in Britain and known universally as the Bren (a combination of Brno and Enfield). It was particularly suitable for jungle warfare, as it was portable and magazine- rather than belt-fed; the imagination does not have to be too sharp to picture the problems of belts of ammunition trailing about in thick jungle undergrowth. Mat Jan in Malaysia had assured me of an order for 4,000 Bren guns if I could supply them in 7.62 mm calibre. I knew that both the British and the South Africans effected very good conversions for the Bren, from .303″ to 7.62 mm. I asked Neethling if South Africa was keeping her Bren guns or phasing them out; if the latter, I would be interested in buying them. My idea was to import them into England, refurbish them at Sterling and remove any South African markings since they would not go down too well in Malaysia. Neethling told me that it was intended to dispose of the Brens, and he would register my interest. Alas, it all came to nothing. South Africa became involved in a war in Angola and realized that her own forces would need the guns. Neethling Coetzee was most apologetic.

He also put me in touch with Anton Hausler, who owned the Hausler Scientific Instrument Company in Jeppe, in Johannesburg. Hausler had been in South Africa for many years, but he was in fact German (and as a result was interned during the war). The company was one of the leading sub-contractors to the Armaments Board and actually produced complete fuses for ordnance. When I first visited them in the '70s, they had a large machine shop full of the very best German and Swiss machine tools. Now there are plenty from Japan as well. In the early days, Hausler told me, he had faced an uphill struggle; even though South Africa was an industrialized nation, aspects of production that we would take for granted in Western Europe or North America – heat treatment, for instance, or certain material specifications – were either sub-standard or very difficult to obtain. Hausler and I got on well, and coincidentally started our revolver projects at the same time. The company produced (entirely in South Africa) a neat five-shot .38" Special revolver called the Republic, which was sold mainly to the South African railway police.

Other guns were produced in South Africa, but the Government was not too keen on supporting them because the quality was suspect (the Sanna sub-machine gun was one of these). However, one South African company that has made a name for itself through its guns is Musgrave. They now produce bolt-action hunting rifles of the Mauser type: excellent quality but far from cheap.

Back in 1961 Sterling had actually won a licensing agreement with the South African Government which would have meant the Mark 4 Sterling being produced locally. At that time, however, international outrage over the Sharpeville shootings was at its height, particularly in Britain. In consequence, the South Africans decided it would be wiser to buy their military equipment elsewhere. Sterling was just one casualty; the Uzi was substituted for the Mark 4, although only some 17,000 were produced. Another casualty was Alvis, whose armoured cars were replaced by those of the French company Panhard. But that, of course, was before my time.

I had two not-so-clever experiences in South Africa. The first began on a flight back to London. I happened to be reading a South African publication called *Man*: not a gay glossy, as the name might suggest, but a general-interest news magazine that usually has an article devoted to firearms. I was thumbing through this when my attention was caught by a feature on the Mamba, a new South African 9 mm pistol. It was Germanic and good-looking, and I thought it might have appeal in Britain and in some of Sterling's traditional markets. I wrote to Sandock Austral, the South African engineering group that made the Mamba, and expressed my interest. Their reply was prompt. Someone closely connected with the project would be in London in early February and would contact me. Sure enough, I was telephoned by one Joe E. Hale, an American by birth, and we arranged to meet in his room at the Tower Hotel in London.

Hale showed me detailed photographs and some drawings. I was impressed by the Mamba's appearance and capacity, and mentioned that it might have a sales potential in some of our traditional markets. He wanted to know where exactly these were. As I explained, our largest single market encompassed most of the Middle Eastern countries, except for Israel whose armed forces had their own sub-machine gun.

Hale erupted. 'I fought for Israel in the Six-Day War, and I'm not having any of our products sold to any fuckin' Arab.' Then he asked what other countries we sold to.

'Black Africa; mainly Commonwealth countries which —'

'I also fought for Rhodesia, and no goddam niggers are going to get this thing either.'

I had had enough. Either he was going into business to make and sell a product, or he was going to play fascist politics. I told him as much, and walked out.

It still sickens me that South Africa and white South Africans might be judged by a creature so wholly unrepresentative of even the most conservative elements.

That was the end of the story, so far as I was concerned. However, some years later, at a shot show in America, I saw that Navy Arms Inc was exhibiting the Mamba. There had been problems with the pistol, over which Navy Arms had helped, but the South Africans had not sustained product development and were running against the might of the American domestic producers. It merely confirmed my strong belief that that was one deal I was lucky not to have made.

The other little problem arose at Jan Smuts airport in Johannesburg, in 1980.

Sterling's agents in Southern and East Africa were Mike Philip and his associates. Mike had been at Oxford and had actually won a wartime rugby blue; he had also been a district commissioner in Kenya. He was very well connected, and had some fine people working with him. It was always a pleasure to do business in his areas. And it was one of his associates, Donald Darroch, who rescued me on this occasion.

Although there was a complete ban on South Africa, the British Government was happy enough to grant export licences for independent sovereign states (though not for the 'Bantustans', the black African homelands). This was despite the fact that the goods were usually shipped by air to Johannesburg and thereafter taken overland to their final destination. In fact the Swazis preferred their goods to be shipped to Port Elizabeth, more than 500 miles south of Swaziland, rather than to Maputo (formerly Lourenco Marques) in Mozambique, which looks much more convenient on the map. The point was that goods arriving through Port Elizabeth stood a reasonable chance of reaching their final destination, which was not always the case with Maputo. Swaziland was just one of the countries on my itinerary for this trip, which had been arranged for me by Donald Darroch. We were also due to visit Malawi, Zambia and Botswana. As usual, I had taken care over the documentation. I had export licences from the British Government; copies of the Home Office letter that authorized me (and 'officers of the company') to carry prohibited weapons; my Registered Firearm Dealer's licence; and import documents from all the relevant countries.

At Jan Smuts airport, I went through the red channel at Customs and explained to the officer on duty what I was carrying and why, adding the request that they should hold the arms in security until they were placed aboard the Swazi Air flight on the following morning. The man seemed puzzled. I told him this was all quite normal; the procedure was the same the world over. I gave him copies of all my documentation, but he was still very diffident. Eventually he called in his superior.

The man who then appeared, dour and unsmiling, was familiar to me. I had seen him on previous visits, although I had never before had to deal with him. His manner was every bit as unfriendly as I had surmised.

'I'm not permitting you to take arms into a place like Swaziland.'

As civilly as I could, I explained that I wasn't taking the goods through South Africa, merely on an over-flight. There was no security risk. But this, apparently, was not what worried him. He repeated that he would not let me take the weapons into 'blerrie Swaziland'. I pointed out that Swaziland was an independent sovereign state, that I was going there to demonstrate the arms to Swazi authorities, and that I had all the necessary permissions to do so.

'I don't care what you've got, man. I'm not allowing those weapons into Swaziland.'

The stubborn refrain was annoying me. I warned him that by questioning my government's authority, and the sovereign status of Swaziland, he could be creating one hell of a rumpus. He didn't care. If I didn't like it, he snarled, I could ring the appropriate government office on Monday.

It was a Saturday afternoon. I was meant to be flying into Swaziland on the Sunday, and had meetings scheduled for Monday morning, with demonstrations on Monday afternoon and Tuesday morning, and then a tight schedule all the way round the rest of the countries. But there was no point arguing. I requested that Customs should take custody of the guns until I had sorted things out. Reluctantly, the Customs official agreed to this and gave me the necessary receipt.

Donald Darroch was waiting for me in the arrivals area and mouthed a few oaths when he heard the problem. Then he propelled me into a car and we sped a few miles up the road to Kempton Park police station.

The South African police have a poor reputation, but it is by no means always deserved. In Kempton Park I found a few very pleasant Afrikaners, interested in small-arms, and the rest mainly ex-RAF, ex-Rhodesia or ex-Malaya. Donald was in his element. He had been in the Palestine police force, in Malaya and in various other British-established police field force units, and knew what para-military police work was all about. He himself was based in Johannesburg although he travelled all around Southern Africa. He chatted to a couple of people, and we were invited to sit down, over a beer or two, while they looked into the matter. It was resolved within minutes, but the police were so friendly that Donald and I stayed for a good two hours.

They were as good as their word. The following morning, the guns were brought aboard the Swazi Air flight. I didn't see the Customs official then, though I spotted him a month later when I was leaving at the end of my trip. We ignored each other.

Africa as a whole was one of the most successful areas of the world for Sterling. Apart from Libya, other customer countries included Tunisia and Morocco, as well as the Commonwealth territories in sub-Saharan Africa, all of which were well-equipped with the ubiquitous gun. In fact, the tour of Southern Africa that had so nearly ended before it began, thanks to the officious oaf at Jan Smuts, turned out to be very successful too.

In Swaziland I met the Commander-in-Chief of the Armed Forces, General Dhlamini (the most common name in Swaziland). Unusually for a black man in authority, he was small in stature. He was also very cultured. However, what most impressed me was that he ordered a quantity of Armalites. Otherwise, except for catching sight of the world's longest reigning monarch in the main street of Mbabane, the white-bearded King Sobuza II, my most vivid memory of that visit was the demonstration to the police and prison service at a shooting range beside Mbabane International airport. One of the prison officers, eagerly trying out the Mark 4 Sterling in fully automatic mode, was using the foresight only — with the result that 9 mm rounds must have been raining down on the airport building with a mini-howitzer effect. Nobody, however, seemed unduly worried.

Malawi's economy, compared with most in Africa, is flourishing. Formerly Nyasaland (until 1964), the country was deemed to have no hope of surviving when the Central African Federation broke up. However, the charisma of Dr Hastings Banda, the first President of independent Malawi, and some bright thinking by British and South African advisers have helped the country's agriculture to prosper. The Malawi people are hard-working and diligent, which has also contributed to the army's reputation for a high standard of training. Brigadier Dzimadzi, who was my chief contact in Malawi, was no stranger for we had often met in England, when he visited the factory at Dagenham. He entertained me in the officers' mess in Zomba, which housed the traditions and relics of the King's African Rifles. At that time, before the new Malawi capital of Lilongwe was finished, both the police and the army had their headquarters at Zomba. I stayed in the Ku-Chawe Inn, which must be one of the world's best-positioned hotels: perched atop a mountain, with a commanding view over the whole of the Zomba plateau. It is also refreshingly cool at night.

On that trip I was too busy to take a break in Malawi, but from other visits I can warmly recommend the trout fishing around Zomba, where the scenery reminds me of Glen Affric in the

Highlands of Scotland. Another spot worth visiting is Nkapola Lodge on the shores of Lake Malawi. The lake is vast, an inland sea but with fresh water; and it is free from bilharzia, the parasitic fluke endemic to so much of Africa. Unfortunately, malaria is a problem here. The local fish, chambo, is a kind of perch − quite delicious grilled straight from the lake. The area is lush, peaceful and almost deserted. Tourists are still rare.

Leaving Malawi, all passengers were stopped by airport officials who wanted to see if we had any kwachas left (the local currency). When it was my turn, they removed my wallet and asked me the same question. Innocently, I said that I had plenty, because I was returning in two weeks' time to see the Assistant Commissioner of Police in Zomba. My wallet was returned immediately.

After Malawi, Zambia. This was my first visit to the country. Donald Darroch and I flew into Lusaka late in the evening, and I was struck by the imposing highway that took us from the airport to the Intercontinental Hotel. But the following morning, when I went out to stroll around, I was rapidly disabused of my first impression. The town was squalid. Most other roads were dirt. The shops had no stock and the whole place was run down. Even the beer was anonymous, as the bottles carried no labels. It tasted good, though − and also strangely familiar. I learnt later that it was Lion Lager, from South Africa.

While in Zambia I happened to run into a friend from the Honourable Artillery Company with whom I had played rugby. David Knights, formerly a professional soldier, was now working for the security printing company, Bradbury Wilkinson. I introduced him to Donald, who asked him what he was doing in Zambia since the Zambians had no money.

'Oh, I'm not seeing the Zambians,' David said. 'I'm seeing Sam Nujoma of Swapo, on the subject of banknotes for Namibia.'

Donald turned away in disgust and walked off with his nose in the air. Although recognized by the UN as a legitimate Namibian political organization, in South Africa Swapo was still regarded as a bunch of guerrillas. Actually, I was rather heartened to see such proof of British entrepreneurial foresight.

Botswana I had visited before, with Mike Philip. On that occasion we had given a demonstration in front of Sir Seretse Khama, his cabinet and his sons. He had been very welcoming and extremely kind to me, and I had been impressed with his adviser, Philip Steenkamp, a Kenyan of Afrikaans descent. At that time there were continuing problems in Rhodesia/Zimbabwe; but Botswana, as a front-line state, had played a sensible and dignified role.

On this visit I was well looked after by Ian Khama, one of Sir Seretse's sons, who had been at Sandhurst. He had looked after me before; but then he had been a lieutenant, and now he was a brigadier. The country, too, was prospering, helped by a large investment programme by the Anglo-American Corporation.

A word about Rhodesia/Zimbabwe would not be out of place. Before I had had anything to do with Sterling, I had visited Rhodesia as a tourist. This was not long after UDI (Ian Smith's unilateral declaration of independence) in 1965 and the country was governed by a whites-only minority. It was a prosperous and happy place, for the white population, and ideal for tourists. Ten years later, when I next visited it, the country was called Rhodesia/Zimbabwe, it had just gone through a bloody civil war, and the British Government was overseeing the first (and, from what I can make out, the last) free elections.

I was appalled by the changes I saw and the tragic stories I heard. On this visit I was accompanied by my wife, and we stayed with an old school friend of hers on a farm near Bulawayo. Sally Norval was a widow. Her husband had died during the civil war, shot with an SLR by his own brother-in-law. They had been out together one evening, patrolling the farm at a time when terrorist activity was at its height. In the darkness they separated, then found themselves facing each other in positions that neither could believe the other had reached. We thought that Sally was crazy to stay on the farm after this terrible accident. She lived alone, with her children, behind heavy security fencing. But she had nowhere else to go, and the farm had happy memories for her. Besides, the place had a strange appeal; it was cattle country, very flat and dry, but the stunted, gnarled trees and thorn bushes dotting the semi-scrubland gave it an austere kind of beauty. It was also quiet and peaceful. Somehow, that made the tragedy of war even more poignant.

The horror of it all was again brought home to me when I visited the British South Africa Police (the British South Africa Company had been the country's former administrators). They had returned a police carbine, the single-shot version of the Mark 4, to Sterling for repairs, but the company was then prevented from re-exporting the gun because of UDI. My visit was by way of being a personal apology. At their headquarters in Salisbury (now Harare) I was welcomed and well looked after by Superintendent Ivan Stitt, who showed me around their whole small-arms operation. He also showed me some grisly photographs of the victims of terrorism and the civil war.

I was interested in Superintendent Stitt's forensic laboratory, equipped with Zeiss electron microscopes whereby spent cartridge cases could be married up with the weapons that had actually fired them; the impression of the firing pin on the primer was an individualistic as a fingerprint. Another interesting department was the police armoury. The SLRs (self-loading rifles, of the FN FAL type) were on general issue and the G-3s of Portuguese manufacture, licensed by Heckler & Koch, were kept for reserve; the police maintained they were not as reliable. To my amazement, they also had a Mark 5 Sterling Patchett sub-machine gun which they had made themselves, by adapting a Mark 4.

There was a locally manufactured sub-machine gun that had been designed by a British immigrant, Mansfield-Scadden, whom I had met some years earlier. At around the time that I acquired Sterling, I had been looking at camless automatic lathes for my other engineering company; we had bought some very expensive Swiss automatic lathes (Habegger), but remained interested in a high-precision East German machine. This was made under licence by a machine-tool manufacturer in Downham Market, Norfolk, called Downham Engineering; the machine itself was dubbed the Logi-Turret. Mansfield-Scadden had been the company's salesman, and we met when he called upon me in London to talk about the Logi-Turret. Learning of my connection with Sterling, he had revealed his enthusiasm for guns and, as he was so interested, I gave him a detailed user handbook for the Mark 4. Perhaps, unwittingly, I laid the foundation for his interest in sub-machine guns, for he then emigrated and found his niche and made his name in Rhodesia. It was quite a feat to design and manufacture a reasonable sub-machine gun in a non-industrialized nation, and at a time of civil war.

Today, fortunately, Zimbabwe seems to have surmounted many

of the troubles that accompanied its transformation into an independent republic. Peace and at least a degree of its former prosperity have returned. I feel that it would probably be a good area in which to set up military small-arms manufacturing. The labour costs are low, there is a good element of engineering expertise available, and the Zimbabweans are non-aligned, free to sell to the whole world – in particular to other countries in the great undeveloped market that is Africa.

Following my tour of Swaziland, Malawi, Zambia and Botswana, I stopped off in East Africa. In Kenya I wanted to see Peter Nderitu of the Police, whom I had met in England. He was interested in sniper rifles, particularly as he ran the police shooting team. The Sterling was certainly no stranger to Kenya. Then I had an appointment to show my wares to the Tanzanian Army and Police. By chance, I flew from Nairobi to Dar-es-Salaam in a private plane belonging to Wilken Tele-communications, a company that was owned by two associates of Mike Philip's, Keith Savage and Bruce MacKenzie. (MacKenzie was the first white member of the Kenyan Parliament.) It was an amazing flight, as the pilot took us quite low over Mount Kilimanjaro. In Dar, along with the pilot and the two others from Wilken who flew with us, I stayed in a huge hotel erected by the Israelis; but the lads from Wilken advised me to watch what I said in the rooms since they had been contracted to install the listening systems.

The following morning I duly gave a demonstration to the Tanzanian Army. Although their equipment had been donated mainly by the Chinese, most of the officers I met had been at Sandhurst and were very friendly. In the afternoon I called on the Commissioner and Assistant Commissioner of the Police, neither of whom I had met before. They advanced towards me, beaming, two huge Africans in immaculate black uniforms, starched white shirts, gleaming leather Sam Brownes and highly polished shoes. But it was their accents that floored me. Both of them spoke with British aristocratic plums in their mouths.

'My dear fellow! How very kind of you to come and pay us a visit! I'm afraid that choice is something we are not faced with. Obviously we would prefer better equipment, but then we don't have to pay for it if it comes from the Chinese, what!'

They were charming. Furthermore, to show their appreciation of my visit, they actually broke their rule and sent me a small order for AR-18s.

From Dar I flew back to London with East African Airways, though there was an uncomfortable stage when I thought I might never get home. The flight was diverted to Entebbe, to pick up a hundred Ugandans; then, to my astonishment, we landed at Tripoli airport in Libya. A small doubt crept into my mind. Perhaps the Libyans bore me a grudge, since they had not been able to have their Sterlings; perhaps they were about to haul me off the plane and pitch me into jail. In fact the plane had landed there simply to disembark the Ugandans, but we were kept waiting for three hours. My small doubt would not go away. Finally it transpired that the Libyans had a quarrel not with me but with East African Airways; the airport authorities refused to refuel the plane until they had been paid, and so we all had to wait for some bank to open its doors. Within a week the Libyans' caution was seen to be justified, when East African Airways went belly-up.

A week later I had some shocking news. The aircraft that had taken me to Dar had exploded while landing at Nairobi airport. Both Bruce MacKenzie and Keith Savage were killed. The cause of the explosion was found to have been a bomb, and the finger of blame pointed at President Idi Amin of Uganda. However, there was another rumour that a well-known figure in British public life, who had conflicting interests in that part of the world, could have been involved. I never did hear the outcome of the police investigations. I dare say the truth of what happened has long since vanished into the deepest recesses of what used to be called the Dark Continent, but some of my associates still have very strong feelings on the subject.

CHAPTER FIFTEEN

Exhibitions

Exhibitions are a regular feature of life in the defence industry, both at home and abroad. They are often an unholy scramble, with hundreds of exhibiting companies all attempting to win the favours of the handful of worthies who are endowed with the power to make procurement decisions. Another danger is that the whole exercise, surrounded by the inevitable hype and euphoria, can degenerate into a lavish and very costly party for the exhibitors. I formed the opinion that personnel from the Royal Small-Arms Factory were sent on exhibitions not primarily to sell but as a reward for good work. However, when approached cautiously, with sufficient preparation beforehand and a lot of effort on everybody's part, an exhibition can be worthwhile.

My first exhibition was the Farnborough Air Show in 1973, where, in conjunction with Jennings & Groves, we were showing the Mark 5 silenced gun with a Scotos night-vision sight attached; the idea was that it would be an aid to airfield security. For some reason the *Daily Mirror* ran a dramatic piece about the gun, with the front-page headline: 'Horror Gun Rocks Show'. (Perhaps it inspired the title of a certain hit musical.) Far from being annoyed at the newspaper's sensationalist article, I worked on the assumption that any publicity is good publicity. This was confirmed by a number of friends who telephoned to ask how I'd managed to square the *Mirror*'s editor. (It was well before the advent of Captain Bob.)

Thereafter, we restricted our appearance at exhibitions to the military ones, except for the first Royal Naval Exhibition which we attended for two reasons. Major Keen was an ex-Marine, and we thought his experience might be useful. Secondly we wanted to support this new venture by M.O.D. Sales. As it turned out, we did get some business and considered the exhibition a success.

Ministry of Defence Sales was a section of the M.O.D. that laboured under a misnomer. Although staffed by civil servants, the department assisted with the sales of all British military equipment, whether or not it had been adopted by the British armed forces; they were not restricted to items produced by the Royal Ordnance factories. Furthermore, their job was not to sell − merely to help those who wanted to sell. For all my criticism of the British Government, the Royal Ordnance factories and the M.O.D. in general, I have nothing but praise for M.O.D. Sales. Their staff gave me unstinting help and assistance, and their marketing information was often invaluable. It was they who mounted the exhibitions to show off British defence equipment, and a first-class job they made of it. Their management and back-up was absolutely professional. Their exhibitions included the British Army Equipment Exhibition at Aldershot, which had been copied from the French Army show at Satory; the Royal Naval Equipment at Whale Island, Portsmouth; and a series of floating exhibitions that were mounted on Royal Fleet Auxiliary ships and sailed to pre-selected parts of the world where a tour had been organized.

The Aldershot exhibitions were attended by service personnel from all over the world. Some of the visitors were from countries to which an export licence for our type of equipment − categorized as 'sharp', meaning that you could 'cut' yourself on it − would certainly not have been issued. Nevertheless, they received invitations along with everyone else; the reasoning, no doubt, was that situations can always change.

The floating exhibitions, or 'floaters' as they were known in the trade, were no different in their aims and criteria from the exhibitions on dry land. What was different was that the exhibitors were all, literally, in the same boat: stuck on a ship in a foreign country. The form was to fly out and stay together in a hotel where the ship docked. One therefore became much more closely involved with fellow exhibitors and rapidly came to know their personalities and companies. There was a camaraderie and a genuine spirit of willingness to help one another − rather like a rugby tour!

Up until 1982 Sterling sold to more countries than any other company in the British defence industry, a fact that reflects credit not only on our products but on our sales efforts too. In total we sold to well over a hundred countries, though I admit this includes some quite small purchases from countries like the Seychelles (population 60,000) who kitted out their prison service with eight Sterlings. But even for a company as successful as ours, the roller-coaster effect of feast and famine was the cause of much nail-biting.

There is as much competition in the defence industry as in any other field, with the extra aggravation that governments can and often do interfere with the normal rules of supply and demand by handing out defence equipment free, gratis and for nothing, merely as an instrument of foreign policy.

At the time, in the 1970s and early '80s, Western banks all seemed to share an enthusiasm for anything to do with what is euphemistically called 'defence'. I never understood why. Selling anything new to the M.O.D. or a foreign government is a long, slow, complicated business: it can take five or ten years, and that is only if the product is successful. Nor did the banks understand the gross unpredictability of the business, the fact that a sudden political change of wind might undermine months or years of work. An order might be placed, accepted, processed and an export licence obtained, then suddenly some incident would lead to the licence being withdrawn.

Moreover, some products require not one but two export licences. This was the case with our Armalite rifle. The design was American and under the terms of the licence agreement we had to seek US Government permission for any overseas sale. This was, of course, in addition to the British export licence. On the whole, the US Government's likes and dislikes were the same as those of Her Majesty's Government, though Uncle Sam tended to be more tolerant than John Bull — for instance, in some of the South American countries, and also in Taiwan where the Brits would not risk upsetting Red China because of Hong Kong.

I admit to having broken the (American) law once, but it was not intentional. Pilkingtons requested the loan of an Armalite AR-18 from us, because they wanted to show their night-vision equipment at a defence exhibition in Beijing (or Peking, as it used to be known). We readily agreed and obtained a British export licence as time was short. The Brits okayed everything and we assumed the Americans had done likewise. In due course, there was a photograph on the back page of the *Daily Telegraph* showing both gun and sight on display on the Pilkingtons stand in Beijing. But our delight was short-lived. Later that same day, Armalite informed us that the US Government had declined to issue an export licence for the People's Republic of China. Fortunately, the US Government accepted that this was a genuine mistake; otherwise I dread to think what the consequences might have been.

Where Sterling did especially well, I think, was in following up all enquiries, however unpromising they might seem. The importance of this was brought home to me by a fortunate early experience involving Crown Agents.

Crown Agents is another misnomer; it is a government-related purchasing service, whose officers work on fixed commission, mainly for Commonwealth countries. In my opinion, they offer the customer extraordinarily good value. On this occasion they approached us on behalf of Sri Lanka, with a tentative enquiry for 2,000 Sterlings. They told us that there was no urgency for the quotation, as the country had no available money, and that the enquiry was a mere formality. However, we quoted immediately, and in three weeks had the order from Crown Agents.

Despite all the difficulties, over the years we built up an exceptional record for overseas sales. Every year after my first three, about 95% of Sterling's production went for export, including some sub-contract presswork that we effected for British companies and some spares for the M.O.D. I felt this deserved official recognition. I therefore applied for a Queen's Award to Industry, in the category of Sustained Export Achievement. For three years running I filled out the application forms, and sent them off to the Department of Trade and Industry who handle the award. To no avail. I couldn't think why they kept turning us down, as the company satisfied all the criteria for continuing export growth. In the meantime, I witnessed the award being granted to the Royal Ordnance factories, to British Aerospace and also to various small concerns whose export records, I was sure, did not match that of Sterling. Three times I wrote to the D.T.I.

and asked why we were turned down, but I did not even receive the courtesy of a reply. Finally I put pen to paper and wrote:

Dear Sirs,
Further to my letters of ... (the three previous dates), is the reason why we have not received the award, due to the nature of our products? Please favour me with your esteemed answer in one word − 'yes' or 'no'.
Yours truly
for Sterling Armament Co Ltd
(signed) J. S. M. Edmiston

The answer came back almost by return:

Dear Mr Edmiston,
Further to your letters of ... (all dates given), for which we apologize for not having replied, the answer to your question is, in one word, 'partly'.
Yours etc.

I forgave them everything on this encouraging revelation that there lurked, within the costive bowels of the British Civil Service, as least somebody with a sense of humour.

One of the 'floaters', aboard the Royal Fleet Auxiliary ship *Tarbet Ness*, was in Colombia. It had been scheduled originally to visit Venezuela, but that country inconveniently decided to hold a general election at the very time the exhibitors would be hoping for ministerial attention. Venezuela had been just one port of call in a long sales tour, and rather than rearrange everything for the other ports, Colombia was substituted for Venezuela.

Along with all the other company representatives, I flew into Bogota and was then flown to Cartagena where the *Tarbet Ness* was berthed. Cartagena is a university town set amid the lush tropical green of the north coast. We were all staying in a hotel just outside the historic and beautiful part of the old town, and the visit began in the usual way, greeting one's fellow defence travellers, many of them old friends by now, and preparing for the two days of demonstrating our 'toys'. Our commercial prowess was immediately tested by the street urchins, who were selling boxes of what purported to be Monte Cristo Havana cigars. The labels were right, just a little faded. In fact the cigars were locally produced, but really quite pleasant, and at ten dollars a box they were good value. However, we found that the boys enjoyed haggling. The most skilled among us was certainly David Gomes, sales manager of the division of Shorts in Belfast who made the world-famous Shorland Armoured Car. Despite his Latin surname, David is as Irish as the day is long, but he turned out to be the past master at street trading.

Both in Bogota and Cartagena we had to contend with quite a bit of thieving. I heard of two or three people who had lost an expensive watch, snatched from their wrists while they were in a car; the thieves were pillion riders on motor scooters, who would dive through the open window of the car when it stopped at traffic lights. A sudden grab, a tug, then they would be gone. I too lost one of my most treasured possessions in Cartagena. I had a pair of shorts, cut down from some very ancient jeans which had faded beautifully. Early one morning, I put them on over my swimming trunks and went down to the main beach for a dip. I was only in the water for a few minutes, but when I returned my shorts had vanished. It was a salutary warning for anyone contemplating skinny-dipping in the area.

The live demonstrations went very well, and extreme interest was shown in the Mark 5 silenced gun. Colonel Roy Smith, the British Defence Attaché, reckoned that I was sure to win a substantial order.

Back in Bogota, where we all homed in on the Colombian defence officials, I was invited to visit the Fábrica José María Córdoba, the military factory just outside the sprawling metropolis with its shanty towns. Colonel Hernán Saavedra Domínguez took me round the plant, where they were assembling Heckler & Koch G-3 rifles and also Smith & Wesson revolvers. Another part of the factory was set up with good equipment and machine tools to produce the American .30″-calibre M-1 carbine. After it had been set up, it was finally decided that the carbine, although a good gun, was obsolete, and so the production line never actually ran. The Colonel was seriously interested in an arrangement whereby he could assemble Sterlings and gradually take on more and more of the manufacturing process of the complete gun. Within hours I received a sample order for both the Mark 4 and the Mark 5 silenced version.

I immediately telexed Beavan Keen in England to apply for an export licence. This had always been the problem with Colombia, even before I bought Sterling. But here I was in the country, on a floating exhibition mounted at great expense by the British Government itself, with the objective of seeking a new market – and furthermore, I had an order. Surely they could not refuse us an export licence now?

They did.

Beavan Keen made some very speedy enquiries and telexed back the result. He had been informed that it was unlikely Sterling would receive the export licence.

Colonel Roy Smith took up the cudgels on my behalf. He told the British Ambassador, who went diplomatically berserk. The British Government was on the one hand encouraging sales but on the other hand refusing to let the sales be completed. Between them, he and Roy Smith ensured that the necessary U-turn be made, though it took nine months. Sterling duly received the export licence for the samples, and they were dispatched accordingly.

But that was not the end of the story. The Colombians then turned round and argued that if it took us nine months to get the export licence for the samples, how long would it take us to supply a proper order? I could see their point of view. Apart from anything else, they had to be sure of continuity of supply. I could not assuage their fears, however much I wanted to. It was, nevertheless, a bitter moment when the assembly arrangement fell through.

I do not know what effect this fiasco had upon the fortunes of the other British defence manufacturers in the Colombian market, but I imagine it gave rise to some discussion among the Colombian military authorities. As it happened, they had also shown a strong interest in Triumph bikes, a gleaming white example of which was also demonstrated at Cartagena. However, at that time the Triumph Motorcycle Co-operative at Meriden had its own problems, albeit of a different nature, and supply might have been troublesome. The Colombians must have formed an odd opinion about the British and their sales tactics. I would not be surprised if they concluded that the British could not be relied upon.

Colombia was a particularly notable débâcle, but it was by no means the only defence exhibition that ended in something less than success. In the early 1980s, we attended an exhibition mounted by American organizers on behalf of Asean (the Association of South-East Asian Nations) in Kuala Lumpur. We did not have particularly high hopes; in fact, we went mainly because we felt that we had an obligation to support the Malaysians, on account of the volume of business we had had in the past with their country.

One of the few interesting approaches I had at that exhibition was from Herr Hambrusch, who worked for Steyr Daimler Puch, the Austrian small-arms manufacturer. He had formerly worked for Deutsche-Merex, an arms trading company in the Middle East, and had bought Mark 4 Sterlings from us in the past. Now Hambrusch was very keen to show me the new Steyr AUG 5.56 mm rifle. I was put off by its futuristic appearance, but it did have an excellent barrel change. It must have cost a great deal of money to tool up, as there were many high-quality plastic parts. However, my major criticism was that it was bull-pup and I have already expressed my very severe reservations about bull-pup weapons. The use the rifle made of plastics showed great technical innovation, and, provided that they can stand up to the extremes of temperature, this is obviously welcome. By contrast, the actual gun technology was as old as the hills; the firing principle was on the good old push-rod-and-rotating-bolt locking system, just like the AR-18. I remember thinking at the time that if the gun became a commercial success, it would be because the customers had confused technical innovation and good cosmetics.

Unfortunately, there was some rub between the Malaysian authorities and the American organizers of the Kuala Lumpur exhibition, and the upshot was that the Malaysian Government effectively boycotted it. In fact, the only small-arms company of any note that succeeded in getting orders out of any branch of the Malaysian Government that year was also the only one that did not exhibit: Heckler & Koch.

CHAPTER SIXTEEN

Storm Clouds

From the defence industry's point of view, the Falklands War in 1982 presented not a sudden surge in orders – it happened too quickly for that – but a practical test for what had hitherto been mere commercial theory.

It was an obscenity and a tragedy to me that two fairly right-wing countries could not settle their differences without resorting to the force of arms. Leaving aside principle, the entire population of the Falkland Islands could have been given one million pounds each and settled in the Outer Hebrides which, I understand, from a geophysical point of view, are similar. With the people out of the way, the territory could have been purchased by Argentina. Were other issues involved?

Tragic as it was, the war inevitably made an impact on the sales of British military equipment. As far as Sterling was concerned, it boosted the demand for the Mark 6 carbine on the American market, as suddenly people wanted to be associated with the victorious Brits. However, in spite of the fact that the late Colonel 'H' Jones VC died with a Sterling in his hand, it was not a Sterling type of war; the shooting distances were too great. In fact, the most successful small-arm that was used (in small numbers) was the old .50″-calibre M-2 Browning machine gun. It was just light enough to carry and proved an excellent antidote to attack from machine-gun posts amid the protection of rock cover – the Browning could actually blast away the rock itself.

Curiously, Sterling had been approached, just before the Falklands episode, with a project that might have made sense in this South Atlantic scenario. The approach was made by a member of the well-known French armaments family, the Hotchkiss-Brandts, and the project, developed only to the extent of general assembly drawings, was a light (30lb) 30 mm single-shot rifle. The major part of the weight was a hydraulic recoil system, and the idea was to be able to fire a standard 30 mm round, albeit with a reduced charge and a shortened cartridge case. It was, in fact, a one-man portable artillery piece with the ability to blast machine-gun nests behind rocks and also to hit helicopter gunships. In certain circumstances — such as those prevailing in the Falklands conflict — it would have been invaluable, but in real commercial terms it was not for Sterling. It was more for a company like British Manufacture and Research of Grantham, who make 30 mm ammunition (at that time they were part of the Oerlikon-Buehrle organization). So far as I know, BMR were never approached, but I understand that the idea was considered by a Middle-Eastern country.

At about the time of the Falklands war, I was introduced to a Syrian, one Husein Al-Ali. He was a businessman from Damascus and was interested in purchasing British defence equipment on behalf of the Syrian Government. This surprised me; hitherto, Syria had been the preserve of the Soviet Union. I checked with the British authorities, to see what the current thinking was concerning export licences to Syria, and was even more surprised when my enquiries met with definite encouragement. Suddenly, from being unacceptable, military business with Syria had become a desirable possibility, although I was warned that nothing of high technology value would be permitted. As I discovered, a sudden frost had iced up Soviet-Syrian relations and Britain was making a deliberate effort to turn this to her own advantage.

Husein Al-Ali interested me, and not just because he did not want any commission added to quotations. Although he would represent Sterling, he was primarily acting for his own government. I had him checked out and was informed that he was an Alaouite (like President Assad) and therefore well connected, and that his brother-in-law was the Syrian Minister of Defence.

On the small-arms side, he was anxious to obtain 5,000 American Ingram small machine pistols with silencers. There was no way the American Government would grant an export licence to Syria for such goods, because of the Israeli connection; however, as it appeared that a British export licence would be forthcoming, the obvious solution was for the Syrians to accept a British equivalent. With this in mind, prototypes of a cut-down Mark 4 Sterling were prepared, to be known as the Mark 7 Para Pistol, with a special silencer. It was not as quiet as the proper Sterling-Patchett Mark 5 silenced gun, but it was as quiet as the Ingram. It was also more accurate than the Ingram.

An export licence was made available without any difficulty, just as I had been assured, and I flew out to Damascus with the sample guns to demonstrate them to the Syrians.

The Defence Attaché was most informative and helpful, and Husein Al-Ali was very good to me. I stayed at the Damascus Sheraton and, when he could not be with me, he laid on a car and a driver (who was armed) to take me around that spectacular and fascinating city. I visited the souks and the Omayyad Mosque. The mosque is a most imposing edifice, originally built as a Byzantine cathedral on the site of a temple consecrated to the Syrian god, Hadad. For Christians, perhaps it is most notable for housing the tomb of John the Baptist, yet it remains one of Islam's most important buildings. The Omayyad dynasty of caliphs had ruled over the Islamic world when it stretched from the Indus to Spain, and Damascus was their capital − until the year 750, when they were overthrown and the new capital of Islam became Baghdad.

The only odd thing about Damascus was that every building, even commercial offices, shops and flats, had a guard or two outside, all dressed in military uniforms and all toting Kalashnikovs. It must have been a significant drain on the economy.

Husein Al-Ali told me that Syria was the Roman name for a province that encompassed not only modern Syria but also the Lebanon, Palestine (as he referred to it) and Trans-jordan. Syria still regards herself as parent to the others, and in particular regarded Lebanon as the English tend to regard Scotland. The fact that Iraq did not support Syria in the Six-Day War against Israel had made them sworn enemies; hence the line-up during the Iran-Iraq war, with Syria (like Libya) supporting Iran. Hence, too, Syria's leading role in the alliance against Iraq during the Gulf war.

The little Mark 7 guns were well received, but the demonstration was a disaster. For the first time ever, I actually experienced feed problems and had some stoppages. It was as puzzling as it was humiliating; the guns had been extensively tested on the Sterling range and had worked faultlessly. When I returned to Dagenham there was an urgent post-mortem. The guns were found to be perfect; the trouble lay with the magazine welding fixture, which through age and use had broken. This had not been discovered before because the broken fixture had not affected the standard 34-round magazines, only the new 10-round ones.

Alas, the damage had been done. It was unlikely that the Syrians would give me a second chance to demonstrate; still less likely that I would get a Syrian order for 5,000 silenced Mark 7s. In desperation, I even looked at the possibility of buying the assets of the Ingram, which then was facing liquidation. However, I would still have to obtain Uncle Sam's permission to export the guns, and I knew this would not be forthcoming. As it happened, Syrian involvement in what they regarded as their province of Lebanon would have put paid to my chances anyway, as the British Government would certainly have revoked my export licence.

After such a promising start, the whole Syrian affair left me rather depressed. No doubt the roller-coaster ride would have brought us better luck next time; but this turned out to be just the first in a string of calamitous events.

The next piece of bad news was that Cyril Olson had died. He used to chain-smoke Ritmeester cigars, and he always kept his office and car air-conditioned to such a low temperature that icicles could form. Whenever I visited him in Singapore, I ended up with a cold. Whether any of this caused his last bout of illness I don't know, but he died of pneumonia. It was a sad loss. He had been a good friend both to Sterling and to me personally.

Meanwhile, trouble had been brewing in my other engineering company, which was run by my brother. The firm was making consistent losses and had an enormous overdraft, but, because of a certain amount of dissimulation over what was happening, and over the true stock-and-asset position, I had been unaware of the magnitude of the crisis that was looming. The bank had tolerated the position since the company was technically the parent of Sterling. But now the company was struggling for its very existence, and the facts could no longer be hidden.

The wise thing to do would have been to close the company down and sell off the machinery. However, I was reluctant to take such drastic action, for three reasons. First and foremost, the staff of seventy or so were extremely loyal, and I did not want to let them down. In fact, I had been intending to introduce a complete product into the firm, but a product and sub-contract work are a bad mix; it probably would not have worked. Secondly, if we did have to let the staff go, we would face an enormous burden of redundancy payments. And thirdly, there was a question over what my brother would do; there was no job for him at Sterling and I could not afford to carry him.

There followed a very painful year of sibling warfare, spawned by jealousy and inflamed by vicious tongues, which ended by damaging both companies, irritating the banks and benefiting only the lawyers. The low point was reached when my brother disputed the arrangement by which my mother had given me the bank guarantee that allowed me to buy the original engineering company. My brother claimed that the arrangement had entitled him to 50% of the shares, not 40%. I eventually found documentary evidence as to the original agreement, and he was forced to back down. By then, however, we had reached the breaking point in our relations. After a series of rows, my brother went A.W.O.L. and I was left frantically trying to run both companies.

Tentatively I looked around for someone to take his place. The situation had become too messy to advertise the company for sale, and I simply could not have coped with all the time-wasters that would have appeared. As it happened, my brother then threatened to wind up both companies. I was given two months in which to buy him out, or the winding-up order would be enforced. As the two months in question were July and August, when half the City of London is on holiday and the other half is not exactly at its most approachable, I was not hopeful of finding the necessary backing.

Furthermore, the situation was complicated by the fact that Sterling was being investigated for its possible part in a contravention of Customs and Excise regulations (see Chapter 18). It was anybody's guess whether or not they would want to prosecute, but our lawyers and accountants quite correctly insisted on a contingent liability being clearly marked on the balance sheets. If the company were found guilty, then what was the maximum penalty that could be imposed? I knew that the company and its officers had acted in good faith throughout, and I was not worried about the outcome if they did prosecute. However, we had to prepare for the worst. It seemed that the worst, in this context, meant a fine that could be a three-times multiple of the value of the goods involved, which in 1982's money meant that a contingent liability of £300,000 was shown on the balance sheet. That figure did not help the earnings ratio. Even harder to swallow was the likelihood that a guilty verdict would leave the company in extreme danger of losing its Section Five Home Office Authority to produce prohibited weapons.

Needless to say, it was a gruelling task to find anyone prepared to offer financial backing for a company in this situation, and in such a short time. What sustained me, I think, was a feeling of responsibility to the labour force. If it were humanly possible, I was determined to keep Sterling going.

In the end I managed to line up three possible solutions to my problem, involving three separate individuals or groups, all of them fully acquainted with the facts that I have described above.

The first solution was for John Varley of Ensign Ordnance quite simply to buy out my brother. John and I would thus be partners. He had been in the Army and had learnt the surplus arms business with Sam Cummings at Interarms, then he had set up his own operation and run it very successfully. He and I had met through Peter Dineley of Bapty & Co, and had become good friends. However, he had been worried about the decline of the surplus market and about the ever-increasing restrictions placed on his customers. He then entered the refurbishing game with .50″-calibre Browning machine guns, but was almost paranoid about employing labour and having the responsibility of a factory. This was the simplest and quickest solution and therefore the one I preferred. John was very enthusiastic about the idea, too, but it all fell apart when he was unable to raise the money on time.

The second solution was the brainchild of Bill Pellew-Harvey and his colleague David Bryens. Again, Bill was a friend of mine; we had met through the defence industry and our wives had taken an immediate liking to one another. He had been in the food business and had had the rug pulled from under him at the wrong moment. However, he had picked himself up and, funded by John Abthorp of Bejam fame, had set up a company called Bonaventure which sold a proprietary range of military accessories. He had, for instance, won some contracts in Libya for targets and ranges, and on the strength of his performance in those had effected further civilian contracts in Libya. The deal he offered was that I should continue to run Sterling with a third of the equity, my brother would be bought out, the engineering company would be disposed of, and Sterling would be backed into a shell public company.

In spite of the contingent prosecution by Customs and Excise, this deal won the formal approval of the Stock Exchange Council. In hindsight, it was a wonderful opportunity to really get going again. At the time, however, it was the solution that I liked the least. Bill Pellew-Harvey had been very kind to me and we had become very friendly. I was worried that I might not be able to perform consistently, as I knew that the investing public is insatiable for growth. The defence game, as I have indicated, was too unpredictable to sustain constant, regular growth. I could not countenance the possibility that I might let a friend down.

There was also the question of Libya.

When the Libyans had been unable to buy their Mark 4 Sterlings, I was approached by a veritable stream of dealers who offered to help me supply Libya using various roundabout routes – for a suitable consideration, of course. Trying not to be pompous, I always explained that it would be against the law to supply Libya, and the penalties far outweighed any possible reward. However, at a later date, one dealer came up with an interesting variation on the theme. He said that the Government of India would supply their SAF carbines to Libya: these were Sterlings, made under licence to India. The restrictions on patents and the conditions of the licensing agreement with regard to third-party sales had expired through the passage of time. Now, apparently, the Libyans wanted to know exactly what differences there were between the British and Indian versions, and they wanted Sterling to list these differences and submit a report on them.

So far as I knew, there was nothing to stop the Indian Government supplying Libya. Moreover, I still felt well disposed towards the Libyans, who had treated me so kindly in the past (and who had not yet developed an apparent taste for terrorism). I was not going to break the law, but if I could help them in some way,

I would. Determined as ever to play a straight bat, I went to the British authorities, explained the situation, and asked how they thought I should respond to this approach. Should I play along, or walk away from it? To my utter surprise, they were keen that I should play along. At least I could tell them, the British authorities, what was going on.

I was flown to India and allowed to test the SAF carbines. They were roughly finished but functioned quite well, though they were not as accurate as either the L2A3 or the Mark 4 Sterling. And, for some unaccountable reason, the Indians had changed the measurements of most of the pins and screws, so that they were not interchangeable with the Sterling parts, although the sub-assemblies were probably interchangeable. I minuted every difference and my report was presented to the dealer in India. The decision then rested with the Libyans, as to whether or not they bought the SAF carbines.

I was then flown home. In due course, I learnt that a shipment of some 25,000 guns was made to Libya. I further learnt, through a third party, that the Libyans were unhappy at the way the guns were packed in thick grease, and even more dissatisfied with the quality. Suddenly I found myself under siege again from the dealers, who this time had the most enormous spares order. What no one actually said, but what was only too plain, was that the Sterling spares would be used to replace the unsatisfactory parts of the 25,000 SAF carbines.

What worried me most about this situation was that it might put too much pressure on Bill Pellew-Harvey. Because he had traded successfully in Libya in the past, sooner or later that tempting spares order would be placed in front of him. In the context of profit-to-earnings ratio it would certainly make an enormous difference to those who were depending on him for results. I simply felt that it would not be fair on him.

Thus, despite its advantages, I backed out of this particular deal.

The third solution involved selling Sterling outright to an Old Etonian gun enthusiast, backed by one David Heiman of Bonus Bonds. He seemed to offer the best hope for Sterling; apart from being interested in and apparently knowledgeable about guns, he was also a chartered accountant. He was very determined to acquire

Sterling, which to me seemed a good sign; when Heiman pulled out, lined up a Swiss-Canadian trust to complete the deal, with himself acting as a trustee.

On the whole, this appeared to be the best solution available at the time − for Sterling at least, and that was my main concern. Just to make sure I had secured the best possible future for the company, I took care to add certain clauses to the sale agreement, binding the new owners to fulfil specific obligations. Even so, I felt nagging doubts as the arrangements went ahead for the sale. I wish, now, that I had heeded my instinct.

CHAPTER SEVENTEEN

A Question of Honour

The sale of the Sterling Armament Company was completed in the early hours of the morning of 23 October 1983, my fortieth birthday. I knew at the time that I was doing the wrong thing, yet the great pose of being able to say that I had retired before I was forty was how I convinced myself to go ahead with it.

Although I expected to maintain a relationship with the new owners, since I had all the contacts and intended to organize orders and act on a consultancy basis to the company, it was sad to be relinquishing control of Sterling. It was an excellent company with a world-wide reputation for quality, second to none. The Sterling sub-machine gun was, quite simply, the best in the world. I had put great effort into the company, and had enjoyed the challenge of building up overseas sales. Moreover, I had had the satisfaction of an excellent working relationship with the staff and employees.

I had always felt conscious of the vicinity of Ford in Dagenham, and the inevitable comparisons in pay. Most of our labour force, at some stage of their careers, had worked for Ford and earned a great deal more money than Sterling could pay. I once asked a tool-maker why he had not stayed at Ford, to which his reply was that whatever they paid, they under-paid, as it was a living hell.

Another interesting remark came from Tom Newton, the shop steward who had been with Sterling all my time and retired when I left. I can remember his exact words. He said: 'We knew you were for real, because when you moved the factory here' — i.e. back to the Dagenham site — 'you had one set of lavatories for everyone, directors, staff and workers alike. That did you more good than you will ever know.' The irony was that I had taken this decision because

I was being mean with the available space, although I admit I always thought that one set of lavatories behoves people to keep them in a better state and makes it harder to steal the lavatory paper!

The annual wage-round meetings had invariably been held in the most genial manner. As I have indicated, I tended to feel threatened by the disparity between Ford pay and that of Sterling. The annual percentage increase, therefore, had to be at least on a par with (if not better than) Ford's and my aim was always to reduce the gap. Tom Newton, however, was always most concerned about whether the company could afford it, and he was often against the young unskilled labour being paid too much. David Howroyd had instituted the excellent policy of having young capable assistants being trained on the job with the older, more skilled and experienced heads of sections. This won Tom's wholehearted approval. He was always keen to encourage any young unskilled employees who showed that they could work hard and in a responsible manner, by offering them the opportunity of learning the skills.

Tom Newton's efforts for Sterling, I'm glad to say, won him official recognition in 1977 − though it came in an unusual guise. That was the year of the Silver Jubilee, when we celebrated the Queen's accession to the throne 25 years before. In industry, the celebrations were marked by, among other things, the granting of awards to various deserving individuals. Thus Tom Newton won the Jubilee Medal. That he should get it, rather than the most obvious candidates − managing director (me) or chief designer, for example − showed a degree of commendable imagination on somebody's part. I was delighted, as indeed was everyone else in the company.

The spirit of the work-force is illustrated by one particular incident that occurred in my time at Sterling. One of the heads of sections, who, as it happened, had not been with the company for very long, had been giving one of the younger employees driving lessons outside of working hours. We then received a complaint from the lad's mother. As far as we could tell, there had not been any actual impropriety, but there was a definite attachment; this was not denied by the older man, who admitted to being bisexual.

Sterling had many employees who were related to each other. In fact, at one time we had six employees all from one family. This was at least partly what people liked about working there: the 'family' atmosphere, the tradition of closeness. But the closeness might conceivably have been jeopardized by this unfortunate relationship. I felt torn. On the one hand, I was emphatic that no employee should be dismissed or victimized because of his private life. On the other hand, we could not shut our eyes to the affair. The older man was sent home, on full pay, while Tom Newton, David Howroyd and I met to talk the whole thing through and decide what had to be done.

Before we could decide on a course of action, however, the man had himself arrested for shop-lifting, then resigned from the company saying that he was 'an old soldier and he did not wish to bring his disgrace upon the company or its directors'.

There are still far too many people in this peculiar country who labour under the delusion that honour is the exclusive preserve of the 'upper middle classes'.

Anything that I made out of the sale of Sterling was gradually dissipated in legal fees − first in the dispute with my brother, then in efforts to compel the new owners to fulfil their legal obligations under the sale agreement. But the new owners of Sterling fell down on their obligations not only to me but to almost everyone else.

I have already mentioned the interest shown in our Sterling revolver by the People's Republic of China, and the deal that I arranged whereby they would have a free licence to manufacture in China while we kept the exclusive right to world sales. The new owners decided to ask for some enormous licence fee, and a royalty as well. Not surprisingly, the Chinese just disappeared. This complete lack of understanding of the market place was only half of the problem. The new owners also refused to listen to any advice.

I left them with a reasonable order for the Saudi-Arabian National Guard, but the situation then degenerated. That was the last order of any real worth that they had. Furthermore, the Swiss-Canadian trust had its own problems, only some of which were financial.

Within a year Sterling was in liquidation. A 'hive-down' was effected and, in a matter of hours, the company was running again. However, with only a tenth of the turnover that we had achieved in my last year of operation, Sterling was going nowhere fast. Yet, as we shall see, just four years later it was bought for an enormous sum of money.

Shortly after this, the Sterling HR-81/83 air rifle was sold to Ray Catt of the American firm Benjamin Sheridan, of Racine, Wisconsin. Peter Moon, the young engineer who had supervised the development of the rifle, went over to set up production in the US. When he returned, he no longer wanted to work under the new regime. He bought into a greengrocery instead; when I last spoke to him he had a chain of six such shops in the area of Medway Towns.

The Armalite, I should add, had long since found a new home. Just before I sold out, Dick Klotzly and Chuck Dorchester of Armalite Inc. had sold Armalite to Elisco Tool Manufacturing in the Philippines (the Colt M-16 licensees). Sterling was handsomely paid off, and some plant and stock, and all the tooling, were shipped out to the Philippines. Chuck and Dick kept faith to the last. They had made only verbal commitments, but they stood by what they had promised, absolutely without any attempt to wring out a better deal or short change in any way. In the context of money and ethics, they outgunned any English so-called gentleman when it came to honour.

In the late 1980s, in its last year of existence at Dagenham, I understand that Sterling witnessed a dramatic cut in staff numbers, to the extent that it became little more than a spares operation. The fact that it was then sold for such a high price merits praise indeed for those in the company who pulled the deal, irrespective of what the effect was on the company itself. As the City keeps reminding us, money is the only yardstick of success.

CHAPTER EIGHTEEN

Guns to Iraq?

It was while I was on a 'floater', a floating exhibition going around the Gulf States at the start of 1983, that I heard that Sterling was being investigated for a suspected contravention of Customs and Excise regulations. In common parlance, the offence was gun-running.

The press reported the story, including a mention of the fact that the Managing Director had 'left the country', implying that I had fled abroad. I knew nothing about the case until it was explained to which shipment all the fuss referred. The irony was that I was actually living aboard a ship chartered by the British M.O.D. which was about to visit the very country to which the consignment had been despatched.

My reaction at the time was that this was patently some mistake. Not for a moment did I believe we had contravened any regulations. If anybody had told me then that I would end up in the dock at the Old Bailey, I would have laughed in his face. Yet that is precisely what happened.

It all began with Reg Dunk. I had been introduced to Dunk in the late 1970s. He was a very tall, bluff Yorkshire-man with a cutting wit. Having set out as a builder, he had decided that arms-dealing was probably more profitable and certainly more exciting. He had discovered that the Eastern Bloc countries were uncharacteristically keen, eager and efficient when it came to the supply of arms and ammunition in their different forms. He asked me to advise him as to what was a representative selection of our products, as a sample order. Explaining that Sterling's range of products then comprised the Mark 4, Mark 5, AR-18 rifle and

AR-18S short carbine, I suggested that the four together would make a good package.

Dunk also asked whether Sterling supplied certain African, Middle Eastern and Gulf State countries. I told him that Sudan had substantial holdings of the Mark 4, along with most of the Arab world; the exceptions could be listed as Syria, Egypt, Algeria and the People's Democratic Republic of Yemen. In most cases, the order had come direct from the country. We had no fixed agency arrangements, but were prepared to act on an *ad hoc* basis. Dunk specifically mentioned Iran and Iraq. The latter, I explained, had purchased a huge consignment of Sterlings, before the British Government had adopted the L2A3; but it was unlikely that they would require any more as their allegiance was now to the Soviet Union. (Incidentally, I had somehow acquired the grisly piece of information that the young King Feisal II of Iraq, who was murdered during the revolution of 1958, had been shot in the back of the neck by a Sterling.) As for the Iranians, they had purchased — of all things — the Israeli Uzi.

I might add that, in the last days of the Shah, Bob Jennings had drummed up Iranian interest in the Sterling Patchett Mark 5 silenced gun, with a Scotos night-vision sight. I did not have much to do with the arrangements, but Bob organized a night-firing demonstration at Ruislip, at Holland & Holland's shooting school. My part in it was simply to meet a party of Iranian generals and the Shah's brother at a Knightsbridge hotel and guide them through London's rush-hour traffic to Ruislip. Unfortunately, no one had told me there would be no room in any of the cars for me, and on that particular day I was driving my wife's miniscule Fiat 500 while she borrowed my smart Jaguar, a prestigious car bought for just such business occasions as this. Nor could she be contacted in time for a swop. I had no option but to brazen it out. I duly met the generals and the Shah's brother and watched them settle back comfortably into their respective cars: one large white Rolls Royce with the number PER 1, and two large black Lincoln limousines. Meanwhile I clambered into the smallest four-wheel car then made and, leading this ridiculous cavalcade, proceeded in a westerly direction towards Ruislip.

The demonstration was a huge success and it turned out that the Shah's brother was very adept at shooting. Three sample gun sets were ordered and despatched to Iran. The recipients were Savak, the Shah's secret police, and I understand that the despatch documentation actually called for the labels to read, 'To the Secret Police, etc, etc' (a shining example of an open secret). Anyway, the vast consignment of three 'horror' guns to Imperial Iran did not stem the tide of change that was flowing, and the rest is history. However, when the Iran-Iraq war broke out, British sympathies — like those of most of the Western and Arab world — lay with Iraq.

Up to this time, further exports to Iraq had been forbidden on account of the Iraqis' close relationship with the Soviet Union. Then I started to receive various enquiries on Iraq's behalf, suggesting that if an export licence became available then an attempt would be made to secure a contract. One such enquiry came through Reg Dunk and his company, Atlantic Commercial Ltd. I did not attach much importance to the enquiries, however, as none of them came from Iraq itself.

One day in the early '80s, we received a rational and straightforward approach from a Major Saunders, who wanted us to supply an order to the Iraqi police. Formerly an officer in the British Army, Major Saunders had also been, at one time, a Defence Attaché in the embassy in Baghdad. We applied for an export licence. Interestingly, it was only refused after a long period of deliberation; the final decision must have been a borderline one. In fact, an opinion was passed by the Department of Trade and Industry that, after a respectable interval, the company might well be advised to apply again. (It must be remembered that, in those days, the heroic forces of Saddam Hussein were ranged against the might of the hated Ayatollah Khomeini of Iran, recently equipped with the best of American arms. The Iranians were the sworn enemies of the Imperialists — that is, the Americans and British — and their lackeys, who included most of the Gulf States.)

Now Dunk put in another enquiry, and was told firmly that an export licence for Iraq was not available. It was always frustrating to be turned down like this, particularly as no reasons had to be given for the decision. On the other hand, because the Government had (and has) the means to judge whether or not a sale was desirable — through the diplomatic and the intelligence services — as well as the power to grant or refuse the export licence, the manufacturer was (and is) relieved of moral responsibility.

Dunk had better luck − or so it seemed at the time − with another order, this one for 200 Mark 5s, ostensibly for Jordan.

Throughout the company's life, Sterling had received irregular but substantial orders for Mark 4s from the Hashemite Kingdom of Jordan. The King and his country held a special place in the esteem of the British Government. Hussein himself had survived Harrow and Sandhurst and had still remained friendly. Although it was well known that the availability of funds for the Jordanian armed forces remained tight, nevertheless an army can usually rise to finance its basic equipment. Various attempts had been made to sell the Mark 5 silenced gun to Jordan, and small quantities had been ordered in the past.

It was therefore not at all beyond the bounds of probability that Dunk's order was genuine. Besides, it came not long after the British Army Equipment Exhibition, where the Mark 5 displayed on Sterling's stand had attracted attention from two Jordanian Army officers: General Hilmi Lozi and Brigadier Fawzi Baj. Coincidentally, just after the exhibition, Sterling was approached by a Jordanian company called Near East Engineering with an enquiry for Mark 5s. This enquiry came to nothing, but the next time I met Hilmi Lozi and Fawzi Baj was on the ro-ro ship in the Jordanian port of Aqaba, where the M.O.D.'s floating exhibition was being held, and the two men asked me how their order was progressing.

It was their order, for 200 Mark 5s, that had come through Dunk.

The first reaction at Sterling, when Dunk's order arrived, was that if it were intended for Iraq it would be a waste of time, as the export licence would never be granted; by then the Iran-Iraq war was well under way. Dunk assured the company that the order had nothing to do with Iraq. He evidenced his order with a certificate signed by the lieutenant-general in charge of logistics in the Jordanian Army, stating that the Mark 5s were intended for the sole use of the Jordanian armed forces. The document was on proper Jordanian Army notepaper and the signature was that of Hilmi Lozi.

Obviously the company could not authenticate this or any other document, but it was submitted with Dunk's order when the request went in for an export licence. In due course, the export licence was granted. The consignment of 200 Mark 5s was already prepared and awaiting shipping instructions when I left England in early 1983 to travel around the Gulf States with the 'floater'. So when Hilmi Lozi and Fawzi Baj met me later in Aqaba and asked about their order, I was able to tell them that their guns had been dispatched.

What I had by then discovered was that, for reasons I did not yet understand, the guns were actually being held by Customs and Excise. An urgent cable had reached me from London, but as yet I knew no details. All I knew was that the consignment of Mark 5s, which had been delivered to the Deep Water Terminal at Greenwich, had been seized and that Customs investigators had also swooped on Dagenham, grilling David Howroyd and Tony Bianco. It was all very puzzling.

After visiting Kuwait, while the floating exhibition made its way round Arabia and up the Red Sea to the Gulf of Aqaba, I flew back to London to take my turn in front of the Customs and Excise. The investigator was very polite and the interview was conducted in a perfectly civil manner. Very soon I was flying out of London again, to rejoin the 'floater' in Aqaba, confident that, so far as Sterling was concerned, the matter had been cleared up and the guns would soon be released.

I was rather taken aback, however, when I arrived at Aqaba and saw, in a huge enclosure just outside the port area, stacks upon stacks of equipment − much of it British − that was plainly labelled as destined for Iraq, including military vehicles painted in Iraqi, not Jordanian, army colours.

It was in February 1983 that the consignment of Mark 5s had been stopped. After my interview, very little was heard from the Customs and Excise. All we knew was that the investigators had also visited Dunk's premises near Doncaster, and had gone through everything from his company books to his underpants. He had apparently kept extensive diaries with his telephone conversations and innermost thoughts recorded in great detail. That was his problem. My problem was that private troubles were affecting the company, and the possibility was looming that Sterling would have to be sold.

I was not even sure whether Sterling had to be involved in any legal action. I therefore made an appointment to see a Mr Silverman, in charge of the Customs and Excise legal department, to ask his opinion. Throughout the 11 years that I had owned the company, I had always been completely open with the authorities. We followed the rules meticulously and, quite apart from our law-abiding natures, there was absolutely no personal or company gain to be made out of gun-running. The order from Dunk had been executed at normal commercial prices. Besides, it was a small order, and it was hardly likely that a company with a reputation as good as ours would jeopardize its own future by acting dishonestly.

All this I explained to Mr Silverman. He listened but would give no opinion. He did not know if a prosecution would take place, nor, if it did, who precisely would be prosecuted.

Thus, for the next 18 months or so, while sibling warfare frayed my nerves and the future of Sterling passed out of my control, I could but wait.

In fact, of course, the wait was a good deal longer that 18 months. In December 1984 (only just inside the period of limitation) the committal proceedings were held at St Marylebone Magistrates Court, London. At the proceedings, a list of charges with the relevant information was heard, so that the magistrate could decide whether or not there was a case to answer; if so, a trial would follow.

By the time of the committal proceedings there was no Sterling Armament Company Ltd; the new owners had run into liquidation. The provision allowed for in the sale price for any possible legal expenditure was gone. The new owners maintained that they had nothing to do with the case, and, although they were using David Howroyd to run their factory, they would make no contribution towards his legal expenses. He was in work and therefore legal aid was not available to him. Although I was not yet working, I agreed to fund his expenses. Since there was no company, the officers of the company at the time of the offences were charged personally.

Dunk was represented by an excellent Queen's Counsel called John Matthews, whom I had met socially some years before in South Africa. He made an impassioned plea on behalf of Roger Dunk, Reg Dunk's son, who had been working in Atlantic Commercial at the time of the Jordanian order, arguing that he should not be prosecuted. We were all pleased when the case against Roger was dropped.

Unfortunately for the rest of us, it was established that there was a case to answer.

The magistrate decided that there had been a contravention of Customs and Excise regulations. It was very borderline, however, and I felt that the magistrate could have exercised a little more authority in the face of Customs and Excise's legal bulldozer.

What compounded our dismay was the doubt over where Reg Dunk stood exactly. He did not appear to be disputing the charge that he had been acting to sell to the Iraqis. His argument was along the lines that other British companies had been dealing in Iraq, including the British Government itself, in the shape of the Royal Ordnance factories and hence the M.O.D. and that he was being victimized simply because he was owed commission on an artillery equipment contract. Apparently there was a difference of opinion as to the rate of commission payable to Dunk. None of this had anything to do with Sterling, however, and it began to seem that the small Sterling deal was being used merely in order to nail Dunk, either for this commission angle or for something else in which he had been mixed up – and this, it turned out, was exactly right.

The trial was set for May and June 1985 at the Central Criminal Court in London, better known as the Old Bailey. David Howroyd and I had a very able young Australian solicitor, John Manuell, who was a great strength during the whole of this ordeal. Our barrister was David Barnard Q.C., a quiet and precise man with a modest manner, quite in contrast with the theatrical pomposity of so many barristers. It was a dry, involved case that hinged on some very fine points of fact and law.

However, before the trial, I was contacted by Customs and Excise. They informed me that if I pleaded guilty, the maximum penalty I would receive would be a £2,000 fine. I told them that I could not nor would not perjure myself. I simply was not guilty of the offence or in any way of misleading the export licensing branch of the Department of Trade and Industry. To plead guilty would be to deny the truth of the matter.

The trial would go ahead. Then suddenly, at the very last minute, matters became even more complicated. Reg Dunk pleaded guilty, on the steps of the court, to the charges laid against him. With the main defendant gone, the trial turned into a farce;

it was, as one defence counsel put it, like playing *Hamlet* without the Prince of Denmark.

The case took a full six weeks. The court would sit from ten-thirty in the morning, break for lunch at about twelve-thirty, reconvene at two-thirty, and recess again at any time after four-thirty. Little wonder it took so long. My wife was much more interested in the juicy rape cases in the other courts, whilst in the court next to ours, some rabbis − all on legal aid, I was told − were being prosecuted for evading Value Added Tax payments on the sale of gold coins. Customs and Excise were after 18 million pounds, apparently: much more worthwhile than our paltry 200 sub-machine guns!

At the outset, the prosecuting counsel, Anthony Arledge Q.C., waved a Mark 5 silenced gun around the court while spouting a mass of facts, some of them inaccurate. The point was never made explicit, but by implication the members of the jury were invited to ask themselves what the hell prohibited weapon manufacture was doing in private hands. I remember feeling sorry for the twelve just men and true (two were women), sitting through this confusing affair that seemed to belong in the realms of Kafka, without even a protagonist (Reg Dunk) on whom to focus. It was a pleasure to tell Mr Arledge, 'with respect' − which in legal parlance means the opposite − where he was wrong in his presentation of the facts. But he had already made his point by waving the gun around. A few weeks later I was to see him acting in a play on television. It is no surprise to me that actors and barristers so often enjoy each other's company in the Garrick Club.

The case was heard before the Recorder of London, Sir James Miskin, or 'Whispering Jack' as he was known by the court officials. He understood exactly what was going on. But all the evidence of the Customs and Excise investigators had to be heard, much of it turgid repetition − which seemed to me to show the witnesses had colluded in assembling it − and, in spite of assurances to the contrary, barely relevant to the case. What lifted the monotony of the court was the intermittent reference to Dunk's diaries, in which he had recorded amusing anecdotes and personal descriptions. His main contact was Khalid Rahal, based in the Iraqi Embassy in London but apparently the Iraqi Army's roving colonel, hovering around Europe to secure supplies, who featured in Dunk's diary as 'our beak-nosed friend, Khalid the Corruptible'.

To me the central point was clear: it simply would not have been in Sterling's interests to break the law. Quite apart from our excellent reputation, which we were always at such pains to preserve, there was the lack of adequate inducement. This case centred on a mere 200 guns, which could never have provided the sort of return to induce anyone to circumvent regulations. In this sort of case, too, it would have been necessary to buy the collusion of several other parties. The mark-up on 200 guns would have had to be so astronomical that the buyer would have baulked at paying it.

Another point that I felt some people missed concerns the destination of the consignment. If the Jordanians had been trying to buy the goods not for themselves but for the Iraqis, and if in fact their end-user certificate was not genuine, then they had pulled off the perfect crime. There was no way that we, as a company, could be expected to see through such deviousness. On the other hand, we had every right to suppose that because the British authorities issued the export licence, they believed the deal to be genuine. If they suspected collusion between Iraq and Jordan, it was they − not we − who had acted reprehensibly in allowing the sale to go ahead.

If one country buys for another, then the goods become the property of the buyer. The buyer is free to dispose of the goods as he wills, unless he has specifically warranted that there will be no such disposal. Even if there is a disposal it is difficult to enforce a warranty. Some years before all this, Jordan had sold a missile system that was 'surplus to requirements' to the South African Government; but, apart from some international teeth-sucking, there was nothing anyone could do about it. In fact, there was usually no point in such a deception, as spare parts from the manufacturing nation are so crucial to successful operation of the equipment.

The great fear, of course, is that one of the nations with nuclear know-how and equipment will export it to, say, Iraq, Libya or Pakistan, and thereby circumvent the non-proliferation treaties. Certain German and Swiss companies have already been under surveillance. In the long term, I am pessimistic. There is a price for everything, even − or rather, especially − between governments. There was even an advertisement, in past editions of *Shotgun News*, for a book on how to make a nuclear bomb.

After the six weeks of interminable legal debate, we at last faced the final agony: waiting while the jury were out. At this point, one of the Customs investigators came up to me and told me not to worry; they had never been after us anyway. Apparently Sterling was the only British firm with which Dunk had done business, but he had obviously upset somebody else and displeased one of Britain's allies, as the order was out to get him.

When the verdict was announced, '*Not guilty*', I felt no elation whatsoever, not even relief that it was over. It was an obstacle out of the way; that was all. The case had cost me a fortune not only in legal costs but in terms of vital time lost in running a new business. Even harder to quantify was the cost in terms of Sterling's value to me. And at the time I did not know what was to be the knock-on effect.

I must admit it was an interesting experience: visiting the Old Bailey as a defendant in a criminal prosecution. It was a minor disappointment that we were not manacled and led into the dock by grim-faced police officers. We came and went with the lawyers, and everybody was very pleasant, including the Customs and Excise investigators and the prosecuting counsel. But it was an experience I would never wish on anyone else. The uncertainty and expense, and the prospect of being branded a criminal, especially when there had been absolutely no criminal intent, had a very draining and damaging effect.

Sometimes, even at the time, I found it hard to believe what was happening. I kept recalling that well-known assertion by the Victorian judge, Sir James Mathews: 'In England, Justice is open to all, like the Ritz hotel.' He was right; justice *is* open to all − so long as one can pay.

CHAPTER NINETEEN

Clues to the Future

Less than a decade later, it feels as though I am writing about ancient history; so much has happened since the days when I owned Sterling. In fact, it is hard to see how a firm such as Sterling could exist in private hands today – particularly in the new Britain created by the remarkable Mrs Thatcher.

The various degrees of private and public ownership can be confusing. Under Mrs Thatcher, many British industries, formerly state-owned, were 'privatized', which in effect meant selling the public's property back to the wealthier members of the public and to the financial institutions. The advantage afforded by this sale of appropriated property lies in being able to draw on human avarice to increase incentive.

The other great confidence trick is known as the management buy-out; that is, companies sell off enterprises to the existing managers who think they are benefiting by acquiring new independence. Why should an enterprise perform better if it is independent? We are told that because management now has a stake, there is a greater motivation to achieve more. I simply cannot believe this. The implication is that British management as a whole needs a personal stake in a company before it can give of its best. If this were the case, then there would be huge schemes assisted by the Government and the Stock Exchange to facilitate the buying of public company shares by their employees. However, sooner or later the managers realize that they have been conned. At first it might be very refreshing to feel independent, to know that destiny is in their own hands. But even at the start, life becomes rapidly more difficult. Suppliers tend to be more nervous and hence exercise a tighter rein on supplies. And gradually the truth dawns. The management is still enslaved, but now to a much less understanding master: the bank. With the high cost of borrowing, it is hard to see anyone in British management today being tempted into a buy-out, unless it is the last-ditch alternative to disposal by an official receiver.

The Thatcher dream or scam, depending on political viewpoint, has already soured; that, ultimately, is why she was forced out of office in 1990. Unless the banks hold their equity on utterly reasonable terms − that is, reasonable in the eyes of reality, which is not the same as reasonable in their own eyes − the situation will become worse. There is already a growing general awareness that the hungry East Europeans, determinedly restructuring their economies as Communism loses its grip, can operate on costs that are a fraction of those in Western Europe. The banks hold the key to our future, and to theirs. The irony is that, at the moment, the hard-pressed home enterprise is subsidizing the banks' efforts abroad; in short, we in the West are helping to create our own future rivals.

A further problem in Britain today, which would certainly make it difficult if not impossible for a company such as Sterling to exist, is the increase in terrorist activity. As a result, the police have become − very correctly − much more demanding about the various security aspects of running such a company, insisting on the highest degree of caution in every movement of arms and on the most strenuous precautions over storage. And naturally the costs of establishing an adequate security system have risen dramatically.

Exporting firearms has its own distinct peculiarities. There are accessories that can be acquired and sold with the original gun, to boost sales and hence reduce overheads. The most obvious accessory is ammunition; without it, a gun's value is purely ornamental. And yet at Sterling we made it a rule to supply ammunition only if we were specifically asked for it. The problem was carriage. Any carrier, or a ship's or aircraft's captain, can refuse to carry arms if he so wishes; but without the ammunition there is less danger, which naturally influences the decision. Also, ammunition is extremely heavy.

But the main factor that deterred us at Sterling from offering ammunition was price. There are too many producers of ammunition, and the profits are extremely limited. Yet this in no way deters governments from entering the field, and the British Government was no exception – at least, not in that respect.

I used to buy 5.56 mm ammunition from Chartered Industries in Singapore, but 9 mm Parabellum and 7.62 mm × 51 mm (Nato) from FMP in Portugal. At the time I was paying the Portuguese an all-in price of approximately £100.00 per thousand rounds for 7.62 mm. Then, when I had a request for some 7.62 mm target ammunition, I visited the Royal Ordnance Factory at Radway Green, near Crewe, to see what price they could quote me. It was a large factory, recently modernized, but so far as I could see it was not exactly flat out with work. The Director announced, as we walked around the 300-acre site, all set about with flower-beds and lawns, that he ran the place at a profit. I could not figure out where the profit came from, and asked the Director what the Government was paying him for normal 7.62 mm ammunition. To my astonishment I learnt that the M.O.D. – and, indirectly, the British taxpayer – was paying £270.00 per thousand rounds.

The Royal Ordnance Factories are now wholly owned subsidiaries of British Aerospace; but the threat of transforming the vast facility at Radway Green into a business park or ASDA hypermarket probably ensures that the Government still pays inflated prices for ammunition.

But if Britain is pricing itself out of the market, there still remains a future for small manufacturers of guns in other countries. Once, when I was visiting Chartered Industries in Singapore, I was introduced to an American engineer called George Frost who had formerly been with Winchester. George had fallen in love in the Philippines and had married and made his life there. He had secured a position with a Filipino company called Squires Bingham, whose main products were .22″ rifles and shotguns and whose largest market was Australia. I was invited to see over the factory on my next trip to Manila. The product catalogue showed a smart modern factory, but when I arrived at the address I had difficulty in deciding whether it was the same building as in the photograph. Apparently it was. The most obvious change was that the factory walls had been removed, and it was not until I went inside that I realized why.

There was no air conditioning. The heat was intense, and the

Filipino labour force were all stripped to the waist with sweat pouring off them. Most were wearing headbands or bandannas, which added to their piratical appearance. All operations were being carried out on manual machines; there was even a manual forging press. I saw not a single automatic or CNC (computer numerically controlled) machine in the place. Hearing me remark on this, George Frost sat me down and explained his philosophy.

If he had installed sophisticated machinery, he would have had to fly in engineers from the USA or Japan or Europe whenever it needed servicing or broke down. He would also lose all the down-time while that happened. However, he argued, the labour rate was so low in the Philippines that he could afford to run and be competitive on standard machine tools. He had also managed to de-skill every operation by providing the operators with go and no-go gauges to the tolerances required; every worker had to perform within those tolerances or he did not get paid. It was a practical and straightforward system, and ideally suited to the industrial conditions of the Philippines. And the result was effective.

There are still too many designers with illusions about CNC machines. It is true that they have improved the cost of running smaller batch production, and there are obvious savings in inventory control; but if a gun product is to be a commercial success it has to sell in substantial quantity. It is also true that the relative cost of CNC machine tools has fallen. However, to achieve competitiveness, the product must be properly tooled, so that the labour-cost element of those both skilled and unskilled is minimized. The tooling and special-purpose machines required to do this can generally be used for nothing else, and, in the event of failure, have only a scrap value. That is not good news to an investor or a bank.

The expertise of gun design can be utilized in civilian or military firearms. For a manufacturer, the ideal is to make something that sells profitably and is not subject to waves and troughs in demand. It was for this reason that I tried to broaden the product base at Sterling. But when I investigated shotguns, I met opposition from Frank Waters, our chief designer. He told me that he would be happy to design any military weapon, but that he had strong reservations about designing anything that was used to shoot birds or animals. He maintained that such creatures can do nothing about their plight; whereas, to some extent, human beings do have a certain control over their lives. Although I enjoy game shooting, and am well aware of the conservation advantages that controlled and responsible shooting brings, I found myself sympathizing not so much with his argument, but more with his personal feelings, and therefore respected them.

There is actually no shortage of good gun designs – or, for that matter, of designers. However, very few of them possess the skill to reduce their ideas to working drawings and proper layouts for economic methods of manufacture. Furthermore, hindsight rather than experience is something that must be forgotten. The tendency is usually to design improvements to past guns, or solutions to past problems, instead of creating something new to meet a new demand. The other trick that few designers possess, but every successful manufacturer must have, is the ability to gauge a product against markets and quantities. It is true that quality alone will always sell, but not necessarily in the quantities that will make it worth the manufacturer's while. A good example of what I mean is the stainless steel revolver made by Korth in Ratzeburg, North Germany. It is beautifully engineered to the minutest detail, but because of this it is also very expensive, which obviously limits its appeal on the market.

Moreover, the timing must be right. In my later days at Sterling I had a meeting with Henk Visser, a Dutchman who lives in Holland but has worked for Mauser and NWM (Nederlandsche Wapen-en Munitiefabriek 'de Kruithoorn' NV) and has strong contacts with the Oerlikon-Buerhle group. He showed me two prototype pistols, good-looking in the Swiss-Germanic style. Henk is a gun man through and through. He owns the finest collection of Dutch duelling pistols anywhere in the world, and so has an eye for a good gun. The very fact that he was enthusiastic about these prototypes was appealing to me; but equally appealing was the fact that the world fashion was just then swinging back to pistols, which would certainly have enhanced their value. Unfortunately, the time might have been right for the world market, but it was not right for us at Sterling.

What all this illustrates is this, that in the civilian gun world there are niche markets and opportunities just waiting to be discovered and fulfilled. Admittedly, it would be extremely difficult to start up without prior experience, and the true profit is always questionable, but a determined individual or group of individuals would survive.

In the field of military weapons, however, it would be virtually impossible – in Britain at least – for anyone to start up today, mainly because of the uncertainty, the time scale and the exorbitant costs involved in marketing and selling. Only the Government can afford to run such an operation, and the Government does not have to make a profit. There was a lesson underlined for me by the M.O.D. itself.

About 18 months after I sold Sterling, I attended an M.O.D. presentation in the main Ministry of Defence building in Whitehall. At the time, the Ordnance Factories were well down the road to privatization and the M.O.D. was out to show that anyone had a chance to compete for Ministry contracts, which in this case involved the second tranche of the SA-80 rifle. There had been some scepticism within the industry that the competition would really be as open as the M.O.D. claimed, but not even the most jaundiced among us would have predicted the outrageous scam they were trying to pull. In spite of the fact that the RSAF Enfield had spent in the region of 100 million pounds taking the gun into production, any new contractor would be provided only with the drawings; he would be expected to lay down plant and tool the whole thing up again. Furthermore, this would only be a sub-contract. No direct foreign sales would be permitted. The whole meeting was an absolute insult to any normal person's intelligence. The quoting exercise alone would cost thousands. There was no help on offer from the Government. On the contrary, the scales were emphatically being tipped in Enfield's favour.

In the end, and to no one's surprise, the product itself turned into a real disaster. This is acknowledged throughout the international gun world, in spite of adamant assertions to the contrary from British officials. The only other country in the world that uses the rifle is Mozambique; and, even though the guns were given to them as a gift, the Mozambique authorities are not happy with them.

It would have been cheaper and more beneficial all round to start afresh, and with up-to-date technology (even if the long-suffering manufacturer bore the whole cost). As always the key is the funding. But if there is a need for a particular product, and there is most certainly a need for a rifle, the M.O.D. could award a contract for the product that most closely fulfilled a rigorously pre-determined specification. That would genuinely encourage competition. It would also avoid the sort of farce that we were subjected to over the SA-80.

Ironically, it was a shotgun manufacturer who put me up for the Worshipful Company of Gunmakers. This is one of the last of the City Guilds that exist to perform a function. The Gunmakers own and run the London Proof House, which, along with the one in Birmingham, has to apply stringent tests to the barrel of every firearm in Britain before it is sold.

I had become friendly with Harry Lawrence, a director of James Purdey Ltd, and had invited him down to Sterling to see how 'machined' guns were made. Although we were at either end of the gun world, he was impressed by the general high standard of engineering. Also, Sterling was one of the largest customers of the London Proof House, as every weapon for export had to carry proof marks.

But even Proof Houses are not infallible. We had some cracked material supplied out of which we made Armalite barrels. The finished guns withstood rigorous test firing and were sent down to the London Proof House, where they sailed past proof (Sterling never had a single gun that failed proof). It was only when they were returned to the factory and examined one last time with an ultra-violet crack-detector that the material fault was discovered. The guns might have been entirely safe, but no one could be sure. All the barrels were replaced and the steel supplier replaced the material with a contribution for the wasted work effort. When we told the Proof House what had happened, they rushed out and bought a crack-detector of their own.

There is another, less obvious service that the Livery Company provide. Because of their position as the Guardians of Proof, the Gunmakers provide an excellent liaison between the military and civilian sides of small-arms manufacture in Britain. Were it not for this, the logical, productive and very necessary contacts between the two would certainly have been broken by the antics of the British Government.

CHAPTER TWENTY

Epilogue

As I have indicated, I had expected to maintain a relationship with the company when I sold Sterling to its new owners in 1983. They knew I had all the contacts, and they knew this meant a lot more than entries in the form of correspondence in the company files. However, when I failed to receive the commission due to me for the first instance of organizing an order and giving the benefit of my consultancy, I decided that it would be wise to distance myself from the company in every way. Besides, in the light of the ensuing litigation, it would not have been fair on the employees to have tried to maintain contact with them, though I continued to have their interests very much in mind.

In the late 1980s the Sterling Armament Company, a mere shadow of its former self, was purchased by Royal Ordnance, a subsidiary of British Aerospace Plc. The consideration is believed to have been very high. The reason for the purchase is by no means clear, though it may have had something to do with the latest product designed by Frank Waters, another 5.56 mm rifle, which had reached the prototype stage. It seems possible that Sterling was bought to close it down. There were those who had been so blinded by the success of our small team, and for such a long time, that they feared the success might be repeated with this new rifle.

What is certain is that Royal Ordnance still cannot believe that Sterling made complete sub-machine guns and automatic rifles *in toto* within the confines of two small factories in Dagenham. And I must admit, looking back, that it does look astonishing; a total of 435 different set-ups were required on the milling machines alone for the sub-machine gun. But the key was the continuous batch production.

In transferring the production facility from Dagenham to ROF Nottingham, the Royal Ordnance 'experts' knew exactly what machines they would take and what had to be sub-contracted. To give an example of how they miscalculated, they invited outside contractors to quote for making the 34-round Sterling magazine; the lowest quotation was for £65. Sterling had last made the magazine for £3 and sold it for £11. Whether or not Sterling had been bought just to be closed down, that in fact transpired as the only available option. The way it was run, it could never have survived.

What saddens me, however, is that at my latest enquiry, only one former Sterling employee was working at ROF Nottingham. Possibly even more worrying is that only six people from RSAF Enfield, who were transferred at the same time, are left in ROF Nottingham now.

Furthermore, a disquieting thought keeps recurring. Perhaps other industries in Britain have suffered the same fate: industries in which we have been or could be world leaders, but which have been destroyed in the same way. On a national level, the results could be calamitous.

Yet even today I know that I could collect a small team, not all ex-Sterling and not all British, who, provided that there was adequate funding, could set up an entirely new, effective and conventional small-arms system without equal in the world. It would take perhaps three of four years to reach full production, but I know it is possible. I have given the subject much consideration, and discussed it with others who share my views. We already have concept drawings of the most important parts. The project could be commercially sound and extremely profitable. Apart from up-to-date technology, we would rely on the same formula that proved so successful at Sterling: namely, a team of the right people, all pulling in the same direction.

Even in Britain, I know we could make it work. We did once before.